HIRING

▲▼▲

HOW *to* FIND *and* KEEP *the* BEST PEOPLE

By
RICHARD S. DEEMS, PH.D.

Career Press
Franklin Lakes, NJ

HIRING
Cover design by Rossman Design
Printed in the U.S.A. by Book-mart Press

To order this title, please call toll-free 1-800-CAREER-1 (NJ and Canada: 201-848-0310) to order using VISA or MasterCard, or for further information on books from Career Press.

The Career Press, Inc., 3 Tice Road, PO Box 687, Franklin Lakes, NJ 07417

Library of Congress Cataloging-in-Publication Data

Deems, Richard S.
    Hiring : how to find and keep the best people / by Richard S. Deems.
        p.   cm.
    Includes index.
    ISBN 1-56414-394-5 (pbk.)
    1. Employees--Recruiting. 2. Employee selection. I. Title.
HF5549.5.R44D34   1999
658.3'11--dc21   98-48155

▲▼▲

Acknowledgments

A special "Thanks!" goes to a number of specific people: my daughter Terri A. Deems, Ph.D., who has graciously and patiently helped me learn more about the next generation and learning organizations; Kathy Kolbe, best-selling author of *The Conative Connection* (now available directly from KolbeCorp in Phoenix), who rediscovered co-nation and whose pioneering work has helped many people understand their natural talents and strengths; Todd McDonald and his coaching in the preparation of some of my earlier books; a host of candidates with whom I've worked including Tom Van Fossen, Dennis Billings, Steve Kastendieck, Nancy Hoppe Johnson, Pete Taggert, David Slaughter, and Becky Stadlman; decision-makers who've challenged me to challenge them, including Gloria Willis, Carol O'Deen, Ken Mishoe, Brad Harper, Kirke Dorweiller, Mike Hoisch, Marilyn Corrigan, Ed John, Bill Neher, Jim Zahnd, Larry Pugh, Bob Deems, Rick Seidler, and Ed Scannel; and the many hiring decision-makers who have asked questions and made suggestions over the years. My aunt, distinguished author Marion Marsh Brown, has been a life-long encourager of my writing and she deserves special recognition for her mentoring. Sandie, who shares my life, receives special "Thanks" for keeping life in balance.

Richard S. Deems, Ph.D.
Scottsdale, Arizona
E-mail: RSDeems@aol.com

▲▼▲

Contents

▲▼▲

▲▼▲

How to Read This Book

This book has been written to be as user-friendly as possible. The writing style is direct and uncomplicated, and the organization makes it easy to move from one chapter to the next. You will find the information easy to apply to your own situation.

To make it even easier to use this book, here are several suggestions on how to get the most from it in the least amount of time.

1. First, take a few minutes to flip through the book, letting your eyes fall on whatever headings or paragraphs grab your attention and reading whatever interests you. Get acquainted with the book and how it is organized. Read the author's comments in the Introduction.

2. Next, turn to the Table of Contents and look at the chapter titles and major topics. As you read the chapter titles, ask yourself, "What chapters seem to address the same questions I have about how to make effective hiring decisions?"

3. Take a sheet of paper and write down the three questions about hiring that are the most important to you now. These are the kinds of questions that prompted you to get this book and take the time to read it.

4. Take your first question and identify a key word, phrase, or topic that might indicate where in this book your question will be answered. Turn again to the Table of Contents and look for that key word, phrase, or topic.

5. When you find that key word or phrase, turn to the chapter of the book that deals with your question and look for the answer. If you are referred to other sections or chapters, read those additional pages, too. Continue until you have your answer.

6. Use this procedure for the rest of your questions. As you find answers you may come up with even more questions. Repeat the process until you are your own expert at finding answers.

If this is a new topic for you, you may want to list your major questions, and then begin reading the book from cover to cover. After each chapter review your list of questions and check those for which you've uncovered your answers. If you're still not sure, take time to re-read a section or chapter. After you've read the book from cover to cover you may want to return to the sections you found most helpful to reinforce the points they make.

The publisher and author hope you find this book insightful and helpful, and that it will be one you frequently pull off the shelf to revisit. The goal is to help you become your own expert at hiring and keeping the best employees!

▲▼▲

Introduction

The successful organizations in the year 2005 will be those that have recruited and hired the best people. In brief form, the team who has the best people wins.

That's usually the case, but in the new millennium there's another factor that must be dealt with. It hasn't had to be considered to the extent that it now has to be considered. The new factor is that there simply aren't enough *best* people to go around. Declining national test scores suggest that many student aren't "learning" as much as previous students, yet they are entering into a decade of increased complexity, more rapid change, and the workplace demand for life-long learning. Those who excell at learning how to think and solve problems will be highly sought after.

Yes, there are a lot of *good* people, and even more *average* people. But best people? Not enough bright people, enthusiastic people, energetic people—employees ready to work, to have fun, and to excel at their jobs.

In order to hire and keep the best employees, you and your organization will need to examine your hiring and managing practices very closely. Otherwise, you may have a full work force but not the people you really need in order to grow, or make a profit, or even stay the same.

In order to compete for the best employees, employers will be required to fine-tune their hiring practices in the next several years—and this book provides new guidelines for redirecting hiring practices in both large and small organizations. It is written for the decision-maker, the person who is responsible for the decision to hire or not to hire. This might be the company president, HR manager, or production supervisor. In any case, all will benefit from taking the time and energy to read and react. People who do the screening will gain new insight into why you do the things you do in order to hire the best.

In those few cutting-edge organizations where the entire work group is involved in the hiring decision the groups will also find in this book the actions to increase their skills in making the right decisions.

This book comes from more than 20 years experience coaching candidates in how to effectively interview, and in assisting organizations in making sense out of their present hiring practices. Showing organizations how to correct hiring mistakes has also been part of our work. We've partnered with organizations to develop recruiting and hiring processes that reduce turnover and enhance effectiveness, and we've helped people identify what they do best so they can describe where they best fit within the organization. At my company, WorkLife Design, we strive to show organizations how to cultivate workplace vitality.

Over the years I've done a great deal of listening to candidates who've reported their experiences in hiring and interviewing situations. Some candidates were treated very well, and the interviewer did an effective job of matching a person's skills with current or future job needs within the organization. In too many instances, however, the hiring process simply excluded good decision-making.

Hiring involves more than just placing an ad, talking with applicants, and making a decision based on some hunch or gut feeling. Your hiring processes are so important that their success is essential for continued organizational viability. Go ahead, read the book. You'll learn.

Chapter 1

▲▼▲

Why Hiring Will Make or Break Your Company

One of the most important tasks you and your company face is hiring. Hiring bright people. Hiring the right people. Hiring the best people. It is so important, I'm willing to predict that the results of your hiring will either make or break your company.

Let's take it a step further: The results of your hiring will determine your company's success in the year 2005—or engage in the "usual" hiring practices of many of today's organizations and your company may not even be around in the year 2005. Do it the right way and you'll be ahead of your competition. Why?

Because the team with the most talent comes out on top.

When you recruit, hire, and retain the best, you're able to anticipate market changes and you will have a work force that is involved in continuous change-improvement initiatives. Your organization will have the people it needs to make the necessary adjustments required to remain ahead of the others. Their energy and drive will enable you and your organization to meet the demands of the next millennium.

If you want to come out on top, you must pause and listen to those who are reminding us that the competition for the best people is significantly increasing. Why? First, there simply aren't enough people to go around. The U.S. Bureau of Labor Statistics projects 151 million jobs by the year 2006 and 141 million people employed. Second, national educational test scores of students have continued to decline. This often shows up as a lack of basic skills for adequate job performance. A 1998 study by the National Association of Manufacturers reported that 88 percent of respondents indicated a shortage of skilled workers and more than half reported employee shortcoming in basic math, writing, and comprehension skills.

Third, not all high school graduates leave public education with a good grounding in computer technology, even though computer technology is such a significant part of today's workplace. In many companies new technology often sits on the shelf because employees don't know how to use it, or are afraid of it, or have no one to train them in how to use it.

Futurist Ed Scannell projects that by the turn of the century the median age of workers will be 45, and by the year 2005 more than 15 percent of the work force will be over 55. It will not be uncommon to find teenagers working side by side with people who themselves have teenaged grandchildren.

What does all this mean? In its "Talent" issue (August 1998), *Fast Company* summed it up: "There are simply not enough truly talented people to go around." Result? Competition for the best people has greatly increased and will continue to do so. "Fast companies make it a point never to 'lose' a talented employee," the editors added. "Talented people may choose to stop working *for* a company, but smart companies know that their job is to keep these talented people working *with* them."

But first you have to get them on board.

That's what this book is all about. Attracting, hiring, and retaining the best people. Before you get started, however, you need to understand why your ability to hire and keep the best people will make or break your company. Here are three reasons why your hiring efforts will either make or break your company in the future.

Only the best deal rapidly with rapid change

If you thought things changed quickly in the 1990s, wait until the next century. *Blur* will be the speed of change. And the difficulty will be in predicting where change will lead or what it will involve. As you've no doubt noticed it is becoming increasingly difficult to predict and prepare for change.

Ever buy one of those greeting cards that plays a song when you open it? That greeting card that you paid two or three dollars for has more computing power than existed in 1950. Thirty years ago the IBM 360 was the ultimate in computer power. Now the camcorder that you bought for several hundred dollars rivals the earlier computers in computing power. My new dual-band, battery-operated phone has more computing power than the first computer used by my company.

What does this mean? I don't know entirely. None of us knows the full impact of all this new and expanding technology. What I do know is that computer technology is growing rapidly. It most likely will have a tremendous impact on my organization and how we get our work accomplished. It cuts costs, adds speed, and increases production. It also adds complexity.

When I sit back and think about technology and the changes I've seen in the past 10 years and listen to technology specialists talk about the future I get exhausted. I can't even imagine all the implications, but what I do know for certain is that computer technology will shape how I get things done in the future. And I'd better be on top of it.

When you hire the best employees, you hire the people who can adjust quickly. This is crucial, because in the next century you will not have time to hire somebody to take care of a new problem that didn't exist a year earlier. The best way to deal with rapid change is to have the best minds on your team so they can *rapidly* deal with *rapidly changing* markets and technology.

Some of the giant corporations are getting behind the curve. Motorola, for some reason, did not anticipate the overwhelming demand for digital portable telephones. For years, Motorola was the dominant supplier of cellular portable telephones. The Classic 5000 was the standard of high-tech and high-quality wireless communication.

But by 1998 that had changed. Digital technology was on the scene and grew very rapidly. According to reports, Motorola sales has declined, its stock value is lower, it laid off 15,000 workers, and it is scrambling to re-establish itself as a leader in portable phones, cellular or digital. The best minds were someplace else, or Motorola would have been ahead of the curve and used its giant resources to take digital technology to even greater usage.

The best way to prepare for rapid change is to have the best people already on board, those who can quickly adapt and make the necessary changes so that the company remains alive and well.

"It is essential that I have the best creative minds available," boasts Relationship Marketing Inc. founder and president Jim Lewis. "Without the best minds I have no one to prod me into new directions, or keep me posted on new technologies, or be ahead of the competition in delivering new concepts and abandoning worn-out ideas, or making sure that I don't get overly satisfied and stop growing."

What are "best minds?"

They are the minds that uniquely combine intelligence, information, and the skill set that enables them to apply information and knowledge to new and emerging problems. Experience in a given economic sector will not be as important as the ability to think and apply information in different ways.

Best people will also have *attitude*, an approach to work in which continuous learning is valued, in which disagreement encourages everybody to grow beyond where they are at the moment, and in which the ultimate goal is to live out one's personal values and organizational values.

Best people will have a drive to find what customers want and value and be ready to work hard to provide that product or service.

Best people will be flexible.

Hiring and keeping the best people is your single most important strategic plan to ensure your survival for the year 2005!

You can't afford turnover

Turnover costs money. Lots of money. It costs to recruit. To interview. To select. To train. And then there are the issues about lost opportunities. What does it cost because a new employee isn't working up to full speed? What revenue was lost because a few widgets didn't get made on time?

When asked how much it costs to recruit and hire a replacement, hiring managers have responded with figures varying from 20 percent to 100 percent of the position's annual salary. What's more important, however, is what it costs you and your organization. Here's how you can do your own research.

Think of a recent and specific situation in which you had to replace an employee because the wrong hiring decision had been made. Take some time to pull your thoughts together. You may even need to ask others for information so you can complete this task.

For each of the following items related to replacing an employee, assign a dollar amount—an estimate is fine. Ask others for their input. Check with accounting. Talk with the managers who didn't make the right hire. And, don't skip over any item just because it takes time to think about the real cost. Each item is important, and each item contributes to the high cost of turnover.

$_____ Decision costs: discussing the situation, trying to figure out how best to handle it, and finally coming up with the decision that a change needs to be made.

$_____ Termination costs, including severance, outplacement, and other benefits.

$_____ Productivity costs: lost productivity and/or lost business while the position is vacant.

$_____ Recruiting costs: newspaper ads, agency fees, lunches, time spent calling other people asking about potential candidates, preparing ads, reviewing job descriptions, and so on.

$_____ Screening costs: responding to phone calls, initial reviewing of resumes, providing information to potential candidates, and selecting "top candidates."

$_____ Interviewing costs: reviewing resumes, developing interview questions, contacting the finalists, scheduling, preparing for each interview, and conducting the interviews.

$_____ Selection costs: evaluating the candidates and making the actual final selection. Be sure you include the several discussions you have with others about how one or two of the candidates might fit.

$_____ Job offer costs: time spent making the offer, negotiating the final agreement, getting approvals for hiring, and setting the start date. Include any moving expenses here, as well as any expenses in arranging housing visits, new office furnishings, and so on.

$_____ Training costs: introducing the new employee to the company, to the work unit, and training the person for the position. Include the costs for orientation programs.

$_____ Learning curve costs: What are the costs because of reduced efficiency while the new employee learns the job? Include any lost-business estimates because that position wasn't filled, or the new employee didn't know how to handle a client, or the new person didn't know how to get the task done right the first time, or whatever.

$_____ Add in here other turnover costs that you've identified but haven't been specifically mentioned above.

$_____ Total Cost of Employee Turnover: Add it up!

This figure is usually much higher than anticipated. Now multiply that figure by all the people you have to hire because the right hiring decision wasn't made in the first place—and you get an idea as to how you can significantly reduce costs. Can you afford this amount each time you make the wrong hiring decision? Most companies can't.

The cost of turnover is a cost that in most organizations can be significantly reduced. By eliminating some of these expenses, there are more funds for new technology, new people, new environment, or lowered costs to consumers or increased return to investors. Reduce your turnover and you can have significant new financial resources to use to further enhance the organization's standing within the marketplace.

What's high turnover? This is the topic of lots of discussion. Some people say it takes 15 percent annualized turnover to keep the company fresh with new ideas and new approaches. Some others say if you get the right people, the fresh ideas keep coming regardless of how long the person has worked in the organization, and that 5 percent turnover is too high.

If you have over 20 percent turnover we at WorkLife Design believe that's too high. You're spending too much time and financial resources just to stay where you are. There is no growth. No excitement. No consistency. No depth in understanding your organization's customers, products, or services.

Hiring the best will reduce turnover. So will effective management practices. My company's own research into the causes of turnover yields results similar to those reported in *Harvard Business Review* and other periodicals. People voluntarily exit an organization because they are having to work too many hours over the traditional 40-hour work week, the physical environment is not safe or pleasing, or they are not managed effectively.

Turnover doesn't just cost dollars, it costs in total organizational effectiveness. The higher the turnover, the lower the total effectiveness of the organization. Even the confidence level of employees goes down when there's high turnover. Think about it for a moment: What would your level of confidence be in your organization if one out of every fifth person hired didn't work out? It wouldn't take long before you'd begin to wonder about all the decisions being made, not just those related to hiring.

In addition, your own productivity would drop as you take time to introduce new people to the right procedures, or you stop to coach the newest employee in how to deal with other departments, or you get tired of working overtime because there aren't enough good people to fill the vacancies. Turnover costs dollars and reduces organizational effectiveness.

You can't do everything yourself

No, you really can't. If your company is to successfully compete and grow, you need good people around you so you can be released to do what you do best—whatever that is. Whether you're a company owner, CEO, department head, or personnel manager, you can't do it all yourself.

"Companies that are in trouble," cautions turnaround specialist Pete Taggert, "are those companies where the owner, CEO, or key managers think they can do everything. They come in at 5 in the morning and leave at 8 at night, and still don't get it all done." For some reason, Taggert adds, these people *think* they can do it all. And they try.

"Seldom are they doing what they do best when they try to do it all," Taggert says, "when what they really need are some good people around them to do the things that need to get done and done well."

A great deal of your own success depends on the people you've brought in around you. If you're smart and wise you've come to know yourself so well, you know what you don't do very well. Those are the tasks that call for others with strengths to compliment your own. It's a sign of strength to be able to say "I don't do these several things very well...and to be truly effective I need others around me who do those several things and do them very well." Strength, not weakness. Wisdom, not folly. Growth, not stagnation.

Sit back and accept that you need other *very good* people around you. Go out and hire the best to complement your strengths. And then be ready to sit back each night and think, "Wow, what a great day! We're all successful together!"

If you know how to hire and keep the best people, then you have good people around you to do the things that need to get done and done well. And you'll be around in the year 2005 to celebrate your successes.

Chapter 2

▲▼▲

Identify What You *Really* Need

Hiring and keeping the best people requires that you know what you *really* need in a position so that you can place the right person in the right job. This takes a lot more than just a gut feeling. Too many times gut feelings result in unnecessary turnover.

Understand the job

To get started you need to know three things: how the job fits into the total organization, the role of the position, and both the technical and functional skills needed to be successful on the job.

Without this knowledge about the job you won't be able to critically identify and select the person who will be successful in the position. As you discovered in the first chapter, when the wrong person gets placed in the job, costs go up, productivity goes down, and it becomes more difficult to hire and keep the best people.

Begin by examining the position at three levels: the organization, the department or work unit, and the job.

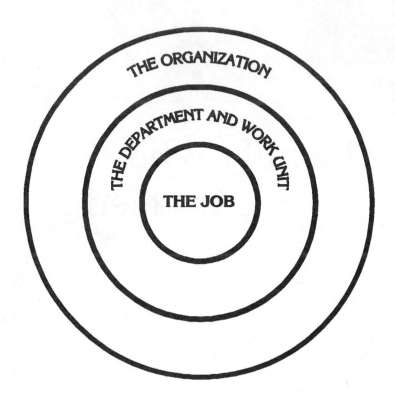

1. The organization

Why does the organization exist? What does it do? How does it go about doing it? Who are its customers? What makes it unique? Take a page and spend the time to prepare a statement about your organization. The statement doesn't need to be fancy or long—it just needs to briefly describe what your organization is all about. Put enough time into this statement because you'll return to it several times during this chapter.

To assist you in preparing your own statement here are three examples:

◄ "Our organization manufactures and distributes widgets worldwide to other manufacturers who use our widgets in producing various gizmos. We use the most up-to-date manufacturing processes available in producing high-quality widgets."

◄ "Our organization provides legal services working exclusively with hospitals, and we get our work done through the combined efforts of attorneys, paralegals, and support staff."

◄ "Our organization develops and monitors marketing plans and materials for non-competing clients from all industries, working together in a highly collaborative environment."

When you can define your organization in a succinct, easy-to-understand, and accurate statement, then you're ready to turn your attention to the department or work unit.

2. The department or work unit

Ask the same questions: What does the work unit or department do? How does it do it? Who are its customers? Here are the three examples:

◄ "Our work unit monitors widget manufacturing equipment to insure its efficient operation and makes necessary repairs so that we can produce high quality widgets; we follow established maintenance schedules and are available for repairs within three minutes of a malfunction, and our customer is the production department."

◀ "Our work unit handles office logistics from answering phone inquiries to typing briefs and all other administrative tasks for the attorneys and paralegals, using a variety of computer-aided tools and occasionally our own foot-power to hand deliver papers on schedule."

◀ "Our work unit develops logos and tag lines for the account executives and assists them in presenting concepts and suggestions to client organizations."

Do you see the progression? See how the work unit's tasks fit in with the rest of the total organization?

3. The job

With this information you're ready to apply the same concept to the specific job for which you'll be hiring. Rather than list all the detailed job requirements, however, at this point you're broadly describing what the job involves.

Here are examples applied to three hypothetical jobs:

◀ "The *maintenance technician* provides scheduled maintenance on all widget production machines, and assists other technicians in making emergency repairs when a machine breaks down, and otherwise insures that production machines are working properly so high-quality widgets can be manufactured for our various clients."

◀ "The *legal typist* provides computer-assisted typing services for up to 10 attorneys and paralegals, insuring adherence to proper format, forms, and terminology; and from time to time may be asked to assist as front-office receptionist."

◀ "The *graphic designer* works in a collaborative work unit assisting the unit in designing logos and developing tag lines; and assists account executives in making presentations to client corporations."

These short descriptions present an overview of the job in uncomplicated words. When you can describe the position for which you'll be hiring in these kinds of terms, then you're ready to add the detail about specific tasks and responsibilities. You'll need to talk with others and do a great deal of listening and observing. Here are three sources for the information you need.

◄ Talk with the employee who currently holds that job, or people who have the same or similar kinds of jobs in your organization.

◄ Talk with those who interact with the person in this position. These individuals usually know what the job involves, and have some very specific thoughts on what it takes to be successful in that particular position.

◄ Review the existing job description.

If the job description hasn't changed any in the past three years then discard it and start all over. Most jobs change, and a job description that's the same today as it was a few years ago is a big red flag. Before going any further, compare your research findings with what the formal job description says. Be ready to revise the job description as new information suggests.

Including too many details in the job description can often deter productivity and effectiveness. Exhaustive, detailed job descriptions have a tendency to produce positions in which people do just what is on the job description and nothing more. As work changes, you cannot change job descriptions fast enough to keep up, particularly if you insist on having every little detail described. Job descriptions that focus on responsibilities and outcomes are more effective than descriptions that list every detail and how the work is to be done. Specific information that will help you understand the job includes:

◄ Does the person manage others?

◄ Does the job involve making decisions relating to policy? Procedures?

◄ Does the job involve technical skills? What specific technical skills?

◄ Does the job involve performance skills? What specific performance skills?

◄ Does the job involve direct contact with company customers?

◄ Does the job involve working with machines? What kind of machines?

◄ Does the job involve relating to other department? What specific departments?

◄ Does the job involve working with any hazardous machines or chemicals? What specific machines or chemicals?

◄ Does the incumbent need to be bonded?

◄ Is this position one in which the successful incumbent will be promoted to the next or a higher level? Are there various "levels" of this position? Do you expect the successful incumbent to move into another department in a few years?

◄ Is there anything else unique about this position?

This kind of information provides a balanced understanding of the maintenance technician position. It not only helps *you* understand the job and how it fits into the entire organization—it can be given to all applicants expressing interest in the job. Once you add the specific technical and performance skills needed to be successful on the job the description can be mailed to the finalists *before* the interview. That way the person comes to the interview with at least a basic understanding of the job and what it involves.

Now you're ready to identify in more detail the technical skills needed for the job.

Identify technical skills

Technical skills are those that call upon specific, technical knowledge, procedures, or manipulation of tools or materials. Examples of technical skills include:

◄ Using specific kinds of machines.

◄ Using specific kinds of computer hardware.

◄ Using specific kinds of computer software.

◄ Manipulating tools in prescribed and precise ways.

For example, the technical skills required to be successful in the widget maintenance technician example might include:

1. Ability to use a PC and common software to prepare reports, establish maintenance schedules, identify maintenance activities on a weekly basis, and maintain parts inventory records.

2. Working knowledge of Wonder Widget production machines.

3. Ability to perform routine maintenance on all models of Wonder Widget production machines.

4. Ability to analyze a malfunctioning production machine and identify probable causes.

5. Ability to repair and correct malfunctioning of all models of Wonder Widget production machines.

6. Ability to use a digital portable phone.

You will need to decide whether previous experience is important for these technical skills, or if you will train the right person. For example, does the successful person really need to have experience on Wonder Widget production machines, or could past experience on similar machines be sufficient to be successful?

Though technical skills are often more easily learned than performance skills, there are many jobs that require previous experience in one or more of the technical skills. Your call.

If the position will be using new or different technical skills in the coming months you must identify those specific skills and provide a general time schedule when those skills will be important. For example, if the widget manufacturer is going to begin using the Great Gee Whiz widget production machines in nine months, and it's essential that the maintenance technician knows how to work on the Gee Whiz machine, then it becomes a needed technical skill. If you'll train the person to work on the new Gee Whiz machine, the ability to learn will be listed later under performance skills.

One caution: If the job doesn't need certain technical skills, then don't list them. Don't get caught in the trap of saying, "Well, gee, if the person had these certain skills it might be nice." If the technical skills are necessary to do the job, then list them. If not, don't bother. Too many job descriptions call for technical skills that aren't used and good candidates are needlessly eliminated. Your review of the position will help you determine what's really needed. Once the technical skills are identified you can focus on the performance skills that are required.

Identify performance skills

Performance skills relate to the tasks and responsibilities assigned to a position and the *way* in which the person

interacts with co-workers, other units, and sometimes even customers. Examples of performance skills include:
◄Managing other employees.
◄Making and being responsible for decisions.
◄Following established guidelines, policies, and procedures.
◄Initiating continuous change procedures.
◄Working closely with other departments or work units.
◄Working with the public, or working directly with customers.
◄Receiving an assignment and reporting on it when completed.
◄Learning new technical and performance skills.

Performance skills are the work habits that reflect the way a person gets a job done as well as the ability and interest in learning new performance and technical skills.

Using the widget example, here is a list of what might be considered the required performance skills for the position of maintenance technician:

1. Work closely and effectively with machine operators and production supervisors and managers.

2. Initiate continuous change processes.

3. Move quickly from routine maintenance work to "emergency" repair work.

4. Stay with a task until finished; for example, emergency repairs.

5. Work as a member of a technical team.

6. Interact effectively with other departments as needed.

7. Learn new technical skills.

There may be a number of intangible performance skills that will make the incumbent successful on the job, such as ability to relate with other departments, handle emergencies, quickly shift from one task to another, and stay with the task until completed. The more you can describe these performance skills, and provide examples, the more clearly you will be able to determine which candidates have those skills.

Are performance skills more necessary than technical skills? You'll need to decide. In some instances both may be needed. In others, maybe there are few technical skills needed, such as the ability to use a computer to send and retrieve e-mail and prepare reports. It depends on the job. I want the technician who works on my car to have many technical skills. On the other hand, the receptionist at the medical clinic better have superb performance skills in dealing with the public.

Once you have identified the performance skills needed to be successful in the position you are ready to match words with needs.

Match words with *real* needs

Sometimes hiring managers use language during the hiring process that doesn't accurately match with either the technical or performance skills required to be successful on the job. This not only leads to confusion in recruiting, but also in making the final hiring decision. Words need to match with the skills necessary to be successful on the job.

Here's an example of using the wrong words to describe a position: ABC Company was trying to recruit and hire manager trainees who would be marketing and selling consumer financial services, such as loans for furniture, cars, and vacations. In their want ads and other recruiting materials ABC Company used words such as "dependable," "systematic," and "objective," because part of the job involved being dependable, following a decision-making system, and not getting emotionally involved in deciding whether to grant a loan.

Instead of attracting people who like to sell, however, they attracted candidates with accounting backgrounds who want to work with numbers. After all, most accountants enjoy being dependable, systematic, and objective. That's their work.

If ABC Company had used terms like "fast-paced," "able to quickly assess and prioritize," and "decisive," they would have attracted the right candidates.

Here's another example: A want ad called for an individual who was flexible, could make quick decisions, and had to meet deadlines. The words they used are words that attract people who tend to work best against a deadline, enjoy working on many things at the same time, and are able to see the big picture.

The position, however, was for a mortgage application analyst—someone who had to sit behind a desk and review lots of figures in order to make decisions based strictly on a formula provided by the company. There was no room for anything other than complete objectivity. Better words? Analytical, objective, consistent, and organized.

Use the right words to describe the technical and performance skills needed in the position and you'll attract the right candidates. If the job involves dealing with irate customers, then say so. If the job involves working late more than 75 percent of the time, then say so. If the job involves heavy travel, then be up front and include it in your statement.

Here are four basic areas of work tasks and functions with accompanying words to match the job needs:

◄ For positions that involve gathering information, processing information, being more of a specialist than a generalist, or making decisions based on having proper information, use words such as:

Practical	Specific
Objective	Thorough
Experience	Knowledge
Research	Information
Detail	Analysis
Prioritize	Allocate
Evaluate	Investigate

You will attract people who are natural information gatherers, and who aren't rushed in making decisions. They will typically remind you of what did and did not work before.

◄ For positions that involve numbers, systems, planning, sequences, trends, or how a process fits into the whole system, use words such as:

Systematic	Consistent
Methodical	Dependable
Coordinated	Efficient
Organize	Structure
Design	Arrange
Integrate	Schedule
Plan	Budget

These people tend to naturally think in terms of how everything fits together. They get more from a flow-chart or diagram than several pages of words, and typically plan for any possible contingency.

◄ For positions that involve taking risks, being innovative, persuasive, selling, making deals, and quickly solving problems use words such as:

Flexible	Challenge
Conceptual	Deadlines
Decisive	Change
Originate	Opportunity
Improvise	Promote
Convince	Varied
Cutting edge	New

These types will eagerly juggle many things at once, and work best with deadlines. These are the people who thrive on change and chaos.

◄ For positions that involve working with one's hands, fabricating, or demonstrating, use words such as:

Mechanical	Quality
Craft	Assemble
Build	Demonstrate
Fabricate	Mold/Form
Construct	Repair

These people prefer a picture to words, and aren't always highly verbal. But give them something to fix, build, touch, or handle, and they won't break it.

As you prepare your descriptions of the technical and performance skills necessary to be successful in the job, check to make sure you're using the right words to describe the actions so the right people will be attracted. You'll reduce the amount of time you spend recruiting, and increase the percentage of people who fit your requirements.

You can also use the words suggested here as you conduct your interview. Also, listen for the words that the candidate uses to describe his or her previous work achievements and experiences.

If you'd like even more information on matching words with real needs, see Kathy Kolbe's book, *The Conative Connection,* available directly from KolbeCorp in Phoenix.

Kolbe's cutting-edge technology can be used as one more resource to match the right people with the right jobs.

Put it all together

You may or may not want to develop an extensive job description. Remember that job descriptions have a tendency to be confining. My own preference is to keep the written description more brief, more global. When you describe a position in more global terms, you get across the idea that the job involves getting done what needs to be done when it needs to be done.

Once you've identified the performance and technical skills needed, you can add those requisite skills to your earlier statement about the company, work unit, and position. You'll have a statement, easily understood by most people who will read it, that gives a clear, concise picture of the position and what it involves. Here's an example:

▲▼▲

Our organization manufactures and distributes widgets worldwide to other manufacturers who use our widgets in producing various gizmos. We use the most up-to-date manufacturing processes available in producing high-quality widgets.

The production maintenance work unit monitors widget manufacturing equipment to insure its efficient operation and makes necessary repairs so we can produce high-quality widgets. We follow established maintenance schedules and are available for repairs within three minutes of a malfunction. Our customer is the production department.

The position of maintenance technician provides scheduled maintenance on all widget production machines, and assists other technicians in making emergency repairs when a machine breaks down, and otherwise insures that production machines are working properly so high-quality widgets can be manufactured for our various clients.

The technical skills needed to be successful in this position include:

1. Ability to use a PC and common software to prepare reports, establish maintenance schedules, identify maintenance activities on a weekly basis, and maintain parts inventory records.

2. Working knowledge of Wonder Widget production machines.

3. Ability to perform routine maintenance on all models of Wonder Widget production machines.

4. Ability to analyze a malfunctioning production machine and identify probable causes.

5. Ability to repair and correct malfunctioning of all models of Wonder Widget production machines.

6. Ability to use a digital portable phone.

The performance skills needed to be successful in this position include:

1. Work closely with machine operators and production supervisors and managers.

2. Follow established schedules and procedures.

3. Ability to quickly move from routine maintenance work to "emergency" repair work.

4. Willingness to stay with a task until finished.

5. Work as a member of a technical team.

6. Interact with other departments as needed.

7. Interest and willingness to learn new technical skills.

With the listing of technical and performance skills completed you can develop candidate evaluation forms for both technical and performance skills. These forms will not only assist you in reviewing the skills needed for the position but will also be useful as you review each candidate's interview and make your final decision. Continuing with the widget example, on the following pages are sample candidate evaluation forms for both sets of skills. Understanding what you *really* need is not difficult to determine when you begin at the beginning—understanding the organization—and continue until you can describe both the technical and performance skills needed to be successful in the position. Remember, your goal is to attract, hire, and keep the best people. Understanding what you need is the beginning. Now you're ready to start attracting the best people.

Candidate Evaluation
Technical Skills

Candidate	PC Skills	Wonder Widget Production Machine	Regular Maintenance	Identify What Is Not Working	Fix What Is Broken	Portable Phone	Other
Ted	Yes	3 years experience	Prepared schedules	Major strength	Works fast	Yes	Prefers self-directed teams
Vicki	Yes, PC at home	1 year experience	1 year experience	Refers to manual	As team member, seldom solo	Doesn't like them	Doesn't like to get dirty
Abdul	Yes, PC at home, programs in Basic	Yes, did computer interfaces to upgrade Wonder Widget	3 years experience with Acme machines	Revised the manual	Better at identifying problems, but can get hands dirty	Yes	Loves machines
Julie	Yes, trained new employees in Word and Access	Familiar, but no direct experience	5 years experience as maintenance tech with Smeed machines	Adept with all kinds of production machines	Yes, "in as little down time as possible"	Yes	The neighborhood fix-it

Candidate Evaluation
Performance Skills

Candidate	Work with Operators, Supervisors, Managers	Continuous Change	Deal With Emergencies	Stay With It Until Finished	Team Member	Interact With Other Departments	Learn New Technical Skills	Other
Ted	Received award for ability to work with others	Identified several major changes to improve quality	Prefers regular maintenance Yes!	"Have to keep the mechanics working"	Worked in teams for past 5 years, enjoys	Likes the variety	Enrolled at community college	Personable, easy to talk with
Vicki	"Everybody has their role and responsibility."	Prefers established procedures	Prefers scheduled maintenance	Not much comment	Prefers to work solo	Can do when necessary	Wants to finish degree in journalism	Seems somewhat inflexible
Abdul	Frequently asked to help solve problems	Designed several new processes as a team member	Thrives on emergencies	Staying past hours is no problem	Facilitated move to self-directed teams	Served on several inter-department committees	Working on certificate	Lots of energy
Julie	Likes to interface with a variety of people and jobs	Enjoys helping team continually assess and refine	Jumps right in	"There are no other options but to get it fixed"	Coached Team effectiveness	Served on several inter-department committees	Wants to take a 6-week Wonder Widget course	Ready for more responsibility

Chapter 3

▲▼▲

Strategies to Recruit the Best

Now that you've identified what you really need in the position it's time to let others know about your needs. Time to gather in the group of candidates who are the best match for the position. You're ready to hire.

Recruiting involves a lot more than just writing good copy for a newspaper want ad. The ability to recruit, hire, and keep the best has to do with the way you run your organization or department. When you have a well-managed unit, the best will be waiting for your next opening. That's your ultimate hiring goal: having a group of highly talented people waiting for your next opening. After all, you can't hire better workers than those who apply.

If you manage your unit the way a lot of organizations manage their businesses, however, you'll not only have expensive turnover but you'll spend lots of dollars on recruiting. Effective recruiting begins with the way you manage yourself and your organization. Following are several actions that can enhance your recruiting efforts:

Position your company in the marketplace

The single most important recruiting strategy is to have the reputation as being one of the leading employers in your field and within your community. That way, when people are thinking of changing jobs, or looking for new challenges, they naturally think of your organization. The best people know it doesn't take any more effort to work for the best.

Establishing this reputation takes time, commitment, and effort. You can't just worry about marketplace awareness whenever you have a vacancy to fill. It is a continuing effort based on your own awareness of your organization's strengths and values and involvement in the community. Positioning your organization as one of the community's leading employers begins at the top and continues all the way down. It's a team effort that involves everyone.

You can enhance your marketplace awareness by following these three strategies:

1. Treat your job applicants with respect.

A good deal of your standing within the marketplace is determined by how well you treat your job applicants. For every applicant that gets treated poorly, there are a lot of people in the community who will know about it before the day is over. There's the applicant's immediate family, family and friends of the applicant's immediate family, and family and friends of family and friends. How many is that? At least 50! Maybe up to 110! And that is too many people out there talking about how poorly you treated an applicant. If one applicant has a bad experience at your organization, you know they will be talking about how poorly they got treated at your organization and why would anyone ever want to work there, and....

Each candidate that walks in and asks to fill out an application or leave a resume needs to be treated with respect and taken seriously. If you accept applications at the main reception desk (and you should), then have a special person designated to talk with each applicant.

"Thank you for thinking of ABC Corp! We appreciate your application and will keep it on file. When a position becomes available for a person with your skills and abilities we'll call. Is there anything you'd like to know about ABC Corp?" That wasn't difficult, was it? You will quickly discover that such an approach has great benefits.

Send a letter to all of your applicants, those who apply in person and those who mail in their resume. In the letter express your thanks for their taking the time to let you know of their skills and experiences and interest in your organization. Tell them again that you'll keep their application on file for the next six months. Include a small folder about your organization: its work, goals, environment, why people like its products or services, and why people like working there.

This is, in fact, a marketing effort. You are marketing your organization as a leading employer so that the best people want to work in your organization!

2. Get some good press.

What the community knows about you is important. What the community reads about you or watches on TV or hears on the radio is all very important to you. It's part of positioning, part of getting recognized as being a top employer.

Why do you think so many executives serve on community and volunteer boards? Is it just their altruistic nature? No! They are getting some good press. After all, who wouldn't be impressed when a local executive not only sends letters about the juvenile diabetes walk-for-the-cure over his own handwritten signature but who is himself out there leading the walk? It's good press. It's recognition. It's building image.

You can build a reputation as a top employer by taking time to get recognized. Maybe it's a special community project the employees get behind. Maybe it's a variety of volunteer projects the employees are already involved in. Maybe it's making yourself available for helpful-hint radio spots. Or a column in one of the area shoppers.

Here are three examples of getting good press:

▲▼▲

Sharon manages three bank branch offices in the western suburbs of a large city. She's dutifully a member of the chamber of commerce, Kiwanis, and serves on the local Y board. But the real recognition she gets for her branch offices is through her weekly column in the local shopper. The column provides helpful hints about family finances, managing money, buying and selling homes, and how to stick within your budget. What really catches the community's attention, however, are her articles about the branch offices' employees.

She includes employees and their stories in the articles. She writes about their hobbies, their volunteer work, and how they make the community better. People read the columns and come to the branch offices commenting about one of the employees, or wanting to volunteer, or sometimes just stopping by to say "Thanks!" for the helpful hint. Why the local shopper? Because shoppers get read.

▲

Jen manages a proprietary school, preparing beauticians and massage therapists for work in their chosen fields. Each term she begins with 65 new learners and asks them to identify potential volunteer projects. As the students get involved with their various projects, Jen keeps the local media informed. A radio talk-show uses them at least once a month to talk about beauty and health tips. Chair massages are given free at the shopping malls on April 15, complete with local TV. Local business offices can request chair massages for entire work teams. The community knows Jen and her school more from reading about her in the paper or hearing her on radio and TV than they do from any advertisements.

▲

Advir is the chief financial officer for a farm supply company with nine regional outlet stores. He had to choose between getting involved within a local country club or serving on the United Way board. He chose United Way. As a board member he gave extra time to help with the accounting and financial management issues not only for United Way but also for member agencies. He took extra time showing member agencies how to more effectively manage existing financial resources and deal with the ups and downs of cash flow. Because Advir had such a great time helping the agencies he was often assisted by other volunteers from his company's accounting department.

He mentioned it in his company's quarterly newsletter, and United Way frequently mentioned the work of his employees in their regular newsletter. The entire community knew about this quiet involvement. Advir gained the reputation of being quietly very competent, and very helpful, and the best began seeking him out as a place to engage their time and energies.

▼▲▼

Getting good press helps position your company as a good place to work. After all, if it wasn't a good place to work how could it get all that publicity?

3. Become the local expert.

A third way to position your organization as an employer of choice is to become a local expert on a business-related topic. Or, you can mentor some of your employees to become local experts. Either way it works.

Take a topic of special interest, such as dealing with rapid organizational change. Interview the top 25 executives in your city about their responses to organizational change, how to lead during change, and what they believe the future changes to be in the next five years. Summarize your findings, and mail each of them a report. Follow it up with a phone call asking if they have any questions or might be willing to add an update in six months.

Then let others know about your research project and findings. Take a copy to your newspaper and ask to meet briefly with the business editor to talk about your findings. Volunteer to be available for an interview, or to add depth to a future story they might be doing. Call the local TV stations and radio talk show hosts and do the same thing. It is important that you accurately report on your research, that you make yourself available at short notice for interviews, and that you assure them you will be continuing to add depth to this topic.

Make yourself available to professional associations and local service groups, such as Rotary and Kiwanis. These groups are always looking for competent speakers on topics of special relevance. If your topic is timely (and it must be), and you can put your thoughts together in a way that keeps listeners' attention, then you will be as busy as you want speaking to various groups.

If you are not a speaker, then you can do one of two things. You can encourage one of your employees to take over this task, or you can learn how to speak comfortably in front of a group. Consider joining Toastmasters. Larger cities have local or state chapters of National Speakers Association. You can also hire a media training firm to train you in dealing with the media. In media training you learn how to be interviewed, how to contact reporters and editors, and how to provide the information you want to get across in ways that attract the attention of viewers, readers, and listeners. Such specialized training is worth the investment.

The more you are perceived as a local expert on some business-related topic the more highly you position your organization as an employer of choice. It's important to have others hear you and then talk about you.

Let others talk about you

The word on the street about your organization can be a very significant recruiting resource. People listen more to what a friend, neighbor, or even the check-out person at the supermarket says, than they often do to a newspaper editorial or news commentator. There is power in the spoken word—or word-of-mouth referrals.

You can get that power working for you and your company. Here are two ways to use word-of-mouth as a recruiting tool.

1. Your employees

Post all job vacancies in a spot where employees can see them. Encourage them to review the vacancies, not only for themselves, but also for people they know. You can establish some kind of referral system, where employees can recommend others they know for posted vacancies. Most organizations reward these employee referrals in a variety of ways: an extra day off, dinner out at a local restaurant, cash, or some kind of catalog gift.

New employees referred by existing employees are usually very good employees. Why? Let's imagine that you read a posting for a new sales manager, and your neighbor Sam, who's also a friend, has had a good track record as a sales manager. You think he'd fit. You recommend him. Before you recommend him, however, you think it through. If Sam does a good job then you're a hero for helping to bring in another top employee. If you think Sam is lazy then you're not going to refer him.

Most employees realize that their reputation is on the line when they refer candidates. Because nobody likes to be put in jeopardy, nearly all employee referrals turn out to be good employees.

When there are special needs, take the time to go to the department or work unit where those needs exist. Talk with the existing employees. Let them know the kinds of people who are needed to fill the positions. Ask for their assistance, and encourage them to suggest the names of people they know who might fit not only the job but also the organization.

How do you get your employees to be your best recruiting resource? You treat them right. Chapter 9, "Keeping the Best," has several suggestions for your consideration

2. Your network

Networking is the primary way people find jobs. The strategy can be applied to finding new employees, too. Keep a list of the professional associations that you're involved in, and some of the key people you know within each group. The next time you have a special need for a special kind of employee, do some networking. Contact some of these people and say something like, "I've got a unique situation in my marketing department for a person to help shape our research efforts. Who do you know that might fit in with my organization? Or who do you know who might know someone who's looking for this kind of challenge?"

Think of the community organizations you get involved with. You can do this same kind of networking with them. You can even network with the professional people you encounter—such as your druggist, your physician, your dentist, and whomever. Just ask. Be sure they know the kind of person you're looking for and follow up on their suggestions.

And let them know what happened. If Sara recommends Tom, but Tom isn't what you're looking for, then send Sara a note: "Thanks, Sara, for introducing me to Tom. His skills weren't quite what we were looking for, but I could refer him over to XYZ Corp." If Sara introduces you to Tom, and Tom is the best thing since sliced bread, then send Sara a note along with flowers or some other appropriate token of appreciation.

You can also network with other companies and your contacts within those companies, even if they are competitors. Call, ask, follow up, and let them know what happened. Be ready to reciprocate when they call you.

Network like this and you'll not only uncover potential candidates but you'll get people talking about what a great place your company must be.

Use want ads effectively

Want ads can still be a useful source of recruiting, particularly when you use them wisely. You can increase your return by taking extra time up front to create the image that attracts the applicants you want.

Your ads should convey a positive image about your organization. Whether it's through an eye-catching logo, layout of the ad, or an appealing tag line (the line that explains the company), your ads should be inviting.

When you maintain consistency in size and appearance, people begin noticing that it's your organization behind those "neat ads." They will take a second look at your ads, hoping that your needs—this time—match their best skills.

What will work for you? Take some time to look at the want-ad sections of newspapers. Let your eyes wander the pages, focusing on those ads that catch your attention because of their appearance. See if you can describe what makes them pique your interest. You don't want to copy someone else's format, but you do want to use some of the same design concepts in your ads.

You can also ask your best people to study the ads and identify those that attract their attention. Ask them to describe to you and others what it is about those ads that catches their attention. With this information in hand you're ready to work with your local papers to design the ads that get the results you want. It may cost more at first, but you'll use fewer ads later on.

Be certain that as you prepare copy for the ads you use the right words. It takes different words to attract high-energy salespeople than it does to attract exceptional customer service people. Why? Because the two jobs call for different skills, and people with different skills respond to different kinds of words. If you haven't read the section on "Match words with *real* needs" in Chapter 2 then do so now. It will save you a great deal of time later.

Want to know where to get the most return from your want ads? Ask your local experts—your best people. Ask them to identify the newspapers that will get to the people you want to interview. Remember that sometimes the shoppers may have the readers you want to attract, and at other times it may be the major newspaper. It all depends on your specific need.

Build an applicant database

Establish a system to evaluate all applicants and add them to a database of potential candidates. For example, you can briefly review resumes and cover letters received in the mail to identify what a person's best skills might be, and where in the organization the person might fit best.

If the applicant showed up in person, have the employee who talked with the applicant make notes on general impressions. Again, review the resume to determine where the applicant might fit, and add him or her to that specific file. The next time you have an opening you can begin your recruiting efforts by reviewing the database to see if top candidates are already on file.

Another way to build this pool is to occasionally run ads specifically for the purpose of increasing potential candidates. Be direct in your ad. Let people know that you are building a pool of possible employees. List the technical and performance skills frequently needed and describe the organization's work environment. Make it easy for people to either stop by, mail, or e-mail their resume.

Again, practice great public relations: Send each person a personalized letter thanking them for their interest in your organization and briefly describing what you'll be doing with their information.

When you have an applicant pool waiting for your next opening, you not only reduce recruiting and hiring costs but you also enhance the status of your organization within your marketplace.

Recruiters and headhunters can help

Recruiters and headhunters may be useful, particularly for hard-to-fill positions and some leadership positions. Although they may cost, there may be times when a good professional placement expert can help.

What's the difference between headhunters and recruiters? Recruiters tend to "market" a candidate by calling their contacts in various organizations to see if they have a need for this special person. Recruiters may be calling a dozen companies to see if they need John or Sally who has these special skills and experiences and "who just might be available in the next few weeks." When the recruiter places a candidate the recruiter collects a fee.

Headhunters, on the other hand, respond to specific contracts or requests for specific kinds of people. For example, if you need a new manufacturing manager you might call a headhunter who will talk with you in detail about the job requirements, skills needed, work culture, kind of temperament that will fit the best, and salary range. Then the headhunter will try to locate the person who can be successful in the job.

The headhunter will then present one, two, or three candidates (depending on what you asked the specialist to do) for your review. If the headhunter is good, you'll have your match in one of those candidates.

Some headhunters will only work on a contract basis— that is, they will only search to find the right person if they have the exclusive contract to fill that certain position. Other headhunters will work on a contingency basis, and hope they are the first to bring you the candidate that gets hired.

When the headhunter finds a candidate that gets hired the headhunter collects a fee.

How much? Fees tend to vary, depending on the market and the level of position, from 15 percent to 50 percent of the employee's annual salary. Headhunters can be useful and worth the expense if you have been unable to find the best people using other means.

Remember that the most effective and least costly recruiting strategy is to position your organization as the best place to work and be successful!

Chapter 4

▲▼▲

Prepare for the Interview in Five Steps

Now that you've identified the skills and experiences needed for the position you want to fill, your efforts turn to gathering information from top candidates. This involves reviewing resumes and asking the right questions during the interview. The interview, the face-to-face encounter between the hiring decision-maker and the candidate, is still the major source of information on which hiring decisions are made. It's essential, then, that you get the right kind of information during the interview—and accurate information.

Here's how you can craft the questions that produce the information you need to make successful decisions:

Step 1: Select your candidates.

You've asked employees to suggest people who might be successful in the position, you've advertised in the local shopper (because that reaches lots of the people you want to attract), and you've reviewed the database for people who've stopped in and left their applications. The stack of applicants seems like a giant mountain.

Now it's time to sift through and identify the people you'll interview.

As you begin the sifting process, think in terms of three piles. The first pile will contain the application packages from those who have been recommended by current employees. Set this pile aside because you will later spend a great deal of time with it.

The second pile will contain those application packages that catch your interest. The past experiences and accomplishments reported by the candidate appear to be a close match to the technical and performance skills you've identified. You'll spend time with this pile later on.

The third pile are all the others. Don't throw those packages away, however. Just because these applicants don't have the skills *now* doesn't mean they may not have just the skills you're looking for in a future vacancy. In addition, you'll want to send each of those applicants a letter expressing your appreciation in their interest, and information about your organization.

Return to the first pile. Because these are people recommended by one of your present employees they have already, to a great extent, been screened. As you review the resumes look for evidence of both the technical and performance skills you need. If your present employee has coached the applicant in the job and the organization, then the resume may look like it was written right off the job posting. It may have been.

That's okay—don't worry about it at this point. It probably means that the person has taken extra time to think about your job needs and whether their best skills match. Usually, people who spend extra time and energy thinking about the job and their skills give extra time and energy to get your job done. If it appears to be a match keep them in the short pile.

Once you've reviewed this first pile take a quick look at those who made it to the short pile. Look again to confirm your assessment that these are candidates you want to talk with. Then get ready to deal with those who didn't make it.

All candidates recommended by employees need extra care and attention. To those who don't make it to the short list, send a gracious "thank-you" letter. This letter needs to express appreciation not only for their interest but also for the interest of the employee who referred them. Here's a sample:

▲▼▲

Dear (Name)

Thank you for taking the time to apply to Widget Enterprises for the position of maintenance technician. We were particularly impressed that (name of employee) had referred you to us, because we value (employee's) recommendations.

There were a number of very good applicants for this position, and though you have many of the skills needed to be successful in this job, there were others who had even more of the skills and experience we are wanting. We will, however, keep your application package on file and will refer to it in the future when we have an opening that calls for someone with your skills and background.

If you hear of a position within Widget Enterprises that you feel you are qualified for, please contact the supervisor for that work unit. Enclosed is our latest employee newsletter and an information brochure about Widget Enterprises.

Again, thank you for thinking of us. We wish you well in finding the place where you can do what you do best in a workplace that provides meaning.

Sincerely,

(Name of manager)

Take the time to personally thank the employees who recommended others. Stop by their work station and personally tell them "Thanks!" for making the referral. If you want, go ahead and *briefly* explain why the person didn't make it to the short list. Encourage the employee to continue recommending people who might fit within your organization.

Your employees will remember this kind of personal attention and will be glad they're working with you. You can bet your competition isn't doing anything like this. It's all part of hiring and *keeping* the best.

You still have a middle pile and it's late and you wonder what to do next. Begin by looking at the cover letter. If the cover letter addresses the qualifications listed in your ad then read on. As you read, look for key words that suggest the applicant has the technical and performance skills needed to be successful.

Look at the job history section and see if there's a progression of titles and/or responsibilities from earlier positions through to the present. If there is, then here may be someone you want to interview. If there's no real progression it could mean the person hit their peak some time ago and aren't progressing further.

If the resume isn't neat and attractive then it suggests the person may not pay attention to detail and may not do the quality work you're looking for. If there is poor grammar it may be an indication that the person doesn't put in the extra effort to do things right, or even lacks the desire to know what's right. Or, in some instances, it could mean the person had a lousy education.

The most common resume is chronological—starting with the individual's current job and working backward through employment history. You may find some resumes that are functional—presenting several major skill areas or strengths, with examples of accomplishments for each heading. When combined with the chronological resume this format provides a considerable amount of information, already organized to make it easier for you to determine if this is a person you need to interview.

Reviewing resumes is not always easy, so don't do it all in one sitting. Try to work in shorter blocks so you stay fresh. Even though it's not always easy, try to use the same assessment criteria for each resume you review.

Once you've identified the people you want to interview, reread their resumes once more. This time, make notes to yourself as to the specific kinds of questions you might want to ask about what's on their resume. Begin to formulate the questions you'll ask each candidate during your formal interview by following the basic guidelines.

Step 2: Follow the basic guidelines.

As you begin preparing your specific questions keep in mind these three basic guidelines.

Avoid "yes" or "no" answers.

Questions that can be answered by a simple "yes" or "no" really don't provide you with much information. These kinds of questions are also frustrating to most candidates, because there's no real opportunity for the person to give you information or let you know why the person wants to be successful in the job. Examples of questions that don't provide valid information include:

- ◄ "Are you familiar with PCs?"
- ◄ "Do you like working by yourself?"
- ◄ "Did you like your last job?"
- ◄ "Have you ever assembled widgets before?"
- ◄ "Can you design a spreadsheet?"

Instead, you want to craft questions that invite the candidate to talk about what he or she has done in the past, or what the person has experienced before doing similar kinds of tasks. The candidate talks and you listen for information you need in order to make an informed decision. Here are more effective, open-ended questions that invite people to talk:

◄ "Tell me how you learned to work on PCs."

◄ "Tell me about a time when you had to work by yourself and how you handled it."

◄ "What did you like best about your last job?"

◄ "Tell me your experience in assembling widgets or something similar to widgets."

◄ "We use a variety of spreadsheets here—tell me about a time when you had to design a spreadsheet yourself."

Ask for specific examples of past performance.

Why? Because past behavior is the most accurate predictor of future performance. If you want to know how a person will probably handle certain situations in the future, ask how the person has handled similar situations in the past.

Instead of asking "Have you ever sold widgets before?" ask how the candidate might handle some future task: "Tell me about the various products you've sold and how you sold them." Keep the questions focused so the candidate doesn't ramble and can provide the specific information you need.

Your questions should invite the candidate to talk about how he or she handled a specific situation or set of responsibilities in the past. Here are some phrases that invite the candidate to talk:

◄ "Tell me about a time when you..."

◄ "Tell me what you most enjoy about your present position."

◄ "If you've ever had to handle a difficult customer, tell me what you did."

◄ "Describe a time when you weren't able to complete an assignment on time and how you handled it."

Because past behavior is the best indicator of future behavior, you want to get the candidate talking about how the person handled situations similar to what the person will be handling in the new job.

Keep your questions focused.

Even open-ended questions like, "Tell me about your best skills," may not produce the depth of information you need in order to make a great decision. Remember to stay focused and ask for specific information. Here's an example: The job involves training and supervising five customer service reps. You're interested in knowing how well the candidate is able to train new employees. Instead of asking something like:

"Tell me about your experience in training."

you can say something like:

"Think back to a new employee you recently trained. Tell me how you trained the person and the results you experienced."

Open-ended questions invite the candidate to talk and increase the opportunity for you to uncover the information you need.

Here's another example: The job involves interacting with a number of other departments and work teams. Instead of asking something like:

"Have you ever had to work with other team before?" you can say something like:

"Think back to a time when you had to interact with other work units so the job would get done on time and on schedule. Tell me some of the problems you experienced and how you solved those problems."

Questions that are based on these guidelines are the kinds of questions that encourage the candidate to provide the information you need to make a good hiring decision. With these three guidelines in mind you are ready to begin crafting questions.

Step 3: Prepare four kinds of questions.

In any interview there are four kinds of questions you will want to ask.

◄ The first, rapport-building questions, helps put the candidate at ease.

◄ As the interview continues, the second kind of question, open-ended questions, invite the candidate to provide information about his or her strengths.

◄ The third, probing questions, are used when you want more detailed and specific information than what the candidate is providing.

◄ Non-question questions, the fourth kind of question, don't end in a question mark, and are a proven strategy to help you gather the information you need from each candidate interviewed.

Build rapport.

The beginning of most interviews is often awkward. The candidate is usually nervous and unsure of what's coming next, and you don't have a feel for how the candidate will respond to your various questions and comments. That's why rapport-building questions and comments help break the ice and get the interview off to a great start. These questions and statements are intended to:

◄ Put the candidate at ease.

◄ Gain the candidate's confidence.

◄ Show that you and the company care about the people who are interviewed.

◄ Help the candidate feel that this is a good place to work.

◄ Get the candidate talking about past performance.

Your first words to the candidate *set the mood* for the rest of the interview. When you begin on a positive note the candidate is much more likely to be open and ready to provide the kind of information about past performance that will help you make a great decision.

Here are two examples of rapport-building statements and questions:

◄ "Hello, Felicia, I'm Jose. Thank you for being so prompt. I enjoyed reading through your resume and I'm looking forward to the time we have together today. May I get you some coffee or a soda?"

◄ "Thanks, Ben, for taking time to meet with me today. Your experience as a solid waste disposal consultant is very interesting and I'm looking forward to learning more about you and your work. Please be seated with me at the round table. Did you have any problems finding the office?"

Introductions such as these will put the candidate at ease. The interview will go more smoothly and you'll get better information.

Using the candidate's name in the first statement you make will greatly help. The interviewee will understand that this is a good company to work for, simply because you cared enough to use the person's name.

The responses to your rapport-builders will also reveal important information about the candidate. For example, if you ask about traffic and the candidate smiles and pleasantly responds, "Well, not much different than usual," that tells you something about the individual's positive attitude. If, instead, the candidate frowns and goes into a long tirade about jerk-face drivers who cut in front of you and on and on, you'll learn that this candidate might have some attitude problems.

The time you spend preparing your rapport-building statements and questions will provide big dividends as the candidate relaxes and begins to more comfortably provide information.

Ask open-ended questions.

The objective of an open-ended question is to invite the person to talk about how a previous task was completed, or a special problem was solved. Your open-ended questions will focus on the technical and performance skills necessary to be successful on the job and the experience the candidate has with these skills. If your question does not extract information about an individual's past performance then it's not a good question.

Here are examples of open-ended questions that get at specific past performance:

◄ "John, this position involves supervising others. Please think of an instance when you had to talk with an employee about increasing the number of widgets packaged each day. Tell me what led up to the incident and what you did with that employee to help him or her improve productivity."

◄ "Anne, this job involves sometimes having to deal with difficult customers. Think of a time when you had to deal with a difficult customer and tell me what you did."

◄ "Jennie, give me an example of a goal you had to set, and tell me how you went about reaching that goal."

◄ "Andrew, describe the most innovative work-related project you ever completed. Tell me how you went about completing that project."

◄ "Terri, tell me the kinds of projects you've worked on as part of a team; now think of the most difficult project and tell me why it was difficult and what you did."

◄ "Bob, tell me about a time when you had to step in between two co-workers who couldn't get along, and what you did to help."

◄ "Melissa, tell me about a time when you were able to improve the quality of the widget because you saw how production could be improved."

As you prepare your open-ended questions, keep referring to the technical and performance skills needed to be successful in that position. Make certain that you're asking only those questions that will provide information about how the candidate has previously performed in similar situations.

Think of some probing questions.

Interviews seldom go exactly as planned and sometimes the information provided isn't in the detail you want. Be ready to probe, to ask for more detailed information. Sometimes the candidate is too nervous, or doesn't understand the kind of information you want, or only partially answers your question. You can prompt the candidate by saying something like:

"Let me give you an example of what I'd like, Mei. You said you enjoyed working with difficult customers. Please take time to recall a specific difficult customer you had to deal with...and tell me exactly how you dealt with that person."

Most candidates will appreciate this kind of probing because it helps them provide the information they need. Let them know you understand it isn't always easy to think of the detail during an interview, and that their extra efforts help you make your decision.

Remember, your probing questions need to be directly related to the technical and performance skills you identified earlier. Imagine you're interviewing for a job in which the candidate needs to work as a team member, regardless of how well the team gets along. Your initial question might be something like:

"Sara, tell me about a time when you had to work as part of team when the team wasn't getting well, and how you dealt with it."

Sara's response might have been general, something like:

"Well, we had two team members who sometimes disagreed on how to get something done. Sometimes they would argue and nothing got done."

You can still get the information you need by asking a probing question something like:

"Sara, it would help me if you could go into more detail. Think back to a specific time when those two people were arguing, and describe what you did to help the team reach their objectives."

Your use of probing questions depends on how specific the interviewee responds to your open-ended questions.

Sometimes you will not need to use many probing questions. With some other candidates, however, you may need to do a great deal of probing to get the information you want. Just remember that when you ask an open-ended question you may need to follow it up with a probing question to get all of the information you need to make a good hiring decision.

Ask non-question questions.

You know from your own experience that interviews tend to make a person nervous. Asking questions in a way that does not end in a question mark, however, makes it much easier for the candidate to respond. Individuals will talk more freely and openly about how they get things done. Instead of asking, "What are your best skills," you might say:

◄ "Tell me what you consider to be your best skills."

◄ "It will help me to get to know you better if you can tell me what you believe are your best skills."

◄ "It will help me if you can describe one of your best skills, and then tell me about a specific time when you used that skill."

Instead of asking "Have you ever had to discipline an employee?" you could say:

"Think back to a time when you had to discipline an employee. Please tell me briefly about the situation, and then describe exactly what you did."

Asking non-question questions may take extra time to prepare. Once you put the concept into practice, however, you will find that people:

◄ Are more relaxed talking with you.

◄ Provide the kinds of information you need.

With your questions all prepared, you are almost ready to conduct the interview.

Step 4: Test your questions.

Once you've developed your questions, test them out. Ask yourself each question and think in terms of how you would respond in an interview situation. Reflect on the kinds of information each of your questions is likely to generate. Then ask yourself, "Is this the information I need in order to make a good hiring decision?" Make your wording revisions as you need.

For example, you want to know how the person handles emergencies. More specifically, you want to know if the person—as the maintenance technician—can drop whatever is being worked on when a machine malfunctions and get it running again, as quickly as possible. Your first open-ended question might be, "Tell me how you handle emergencies." You realize, however, that you've not been specific enough. The person can tell you about any kinds of emergencies, job-related or not.

You revise your questions and decide to ask a non-question question: "Though we hope it never happens we all know that Wonder Widget production machines sometimes stop working. It would help me if you could describe a time when one of the machines you maintained malfunctioned and how you handled it."

Much better, you realize.

You can also turn to your local, internal experts—your present employees—and review with them your planned interview questions. Share with them the questions you're going to ask and let them assist you in determining if any revisions need to be made. Because these are the people doing the work, or working with the person who will be doing the work, they are aware of how they would answer questions. They can tell you if you're going to get the information you need. They may even have some questions they believe should be included that you hadn't thought about.

Step 5: Prepare the interview environment.

Your final step in getting ready for the interview is to prepare the interviewing room. If you have a room that's set aside just for interviewing, that's good.

If you don't have a dedicated interview room, then make certain you take time to prepare whatever room you'll use. You will want it to be neat and not cluttered. Boxes of material should either be taken somewhere else or at least stacked in an organized fashion. Any confidential papers or proprietary information should be set aside.

Is the interviewing room private? Too much outside noise is a distraction, and keeps most candidates from talking about what they do best. Noise makes it difficult for both you and the candidate to concentrate.

A round table where both of you can sit is the preferred seating arrangement. If you're in a conference room with a long table, then sit on one side and let the candidate take the chair at the head of the table. If you have to sit at your desk, then seat yourself so that you are not unduly intimidating to the candidate. Anything you can do to put the person at ease will help you gather the information you need.

You are also part of the interview environment and you need to make certain you're prepared. If you get nervous before conducting an interview, take time to walk yourself through an imaginary great interview. Visualize yourself being in control, not at all nervous, asking good questions, and gathering the information you need. Enlist help from some of your co-workers. Ask them to practice with you and conduct a mock interview. Practice until you feel comfortable managing a typical interview. Get feedback from your co-workers to enhance your skills and confidence in conducting effective interviews.

Now that you've taken time to prepare for the interview, it's time for action.

▲▼▲

Chapter 5

The Interview: Get the Information You Need

You may get a hunch that one candidate is a standout as you look at resumes—but not many hiring decisions are made without some kind of interview. It's part of the process. After all, you will be working face-to-face with this person and it's important to have that direct, personal contact before making the final decision.

The purpose of the interview is to give you information that doesn't come across on a piece of paper. During the interview you have the opportunity to ask for details, and learn how the person has handled similar kinds of activities that are involved in th position. You also have the opportunity to assess how the person will probably relate and work with you and others on the job.

Here are 15 actions you can take to get the information you need.

1. Look professional.

You and your attire are also part of the office setting and you will want to be dressed appropriately. What is appropriate? It's situational. If you're interviewing for a senior manager then you'll want to dress as a senior manager. On the other hand, just because you are interviewing for a route driver doesn't mean you need to dress as a route driver unless that's how you dress for your regular work day.

With the emphasis on casual business attire you still need to remember that how you look will have an impact on the information you get and the "feel" the candidate has for the organization. Take a look in the mirror and ask yourself, "Would I want to work for a company where decision makers dress like this all the time?" Make whatever changes you need to.

Your appearance reflects company image. Candidates will find your organization of interest when you look the part of the professional.

2. Make it easy for candidates to talk.

Remember that your success in selecting the best is your ability to get each candidate to talk. To do this you'll want the candidate to feel relaxed and ready to discuss how he or she can meet those needs.

Most candidates, however, come into the interview with fear and trepidation. They're nervous. Uncomfortable with talking about themselves and their accomplishments. To get the information you need, your first action is to make it easy for candidates to talk. Only when the candidate gives you enough information can you make a truly effective decision.

Take one last look at the interviewing room and make sure it's clean, quiet, and invites the interviewee to talk.

Make sure that others know you're in an important meeting and should not be interrupted unless it simply can't wait. Nothing stifles a good discussion more than an interruption.

3. Address the candidate by name.

Your first direct contact with the candidate will also determine whether the candidate will "open up" during the interview. One of the most effective ways to do this is to use the candidate's name. As you shake hands, look the person in the eyes and say something like, "Jeanette, I'm Dick Deems and I'm very glad to meet you. Thank you for coming to our offices this morning!" Start with an introduction like that and you're well on your way to putting the person at ease, and getting them to share the information you need.

If your company is like most companies, you'll use the person's first name. If your company is more formal, then the person's last name might be used. The important thing is to establish quickly that the candidate is regarded as a unique person, with a name, and you know the person's name without having to look at a piece of paper all the time.

4. Start with small talk.

Continue to build a comfort level between yourself and the candidate by "easing into" the interview with some transitional small talk. Mention the weather, the candidate's success in finding the office, acknowledgment that you went to the same school, belong to the same organizations, etc. You can say something like:

◄ "Brad, did you have any trouble on that 20th Street intersection? I know when I moved here it took me awhile to get used to making the right turn."

◄ "Brad, I don't know about you, but I've just about shoveled enough snow for one season."

Look for a connection or mutual interest and start with something like this:

◄ "Betsy, I'm very glad to meet you. I've seen you at Toastmasters and I'm looking forward to our meeting this morning. Tell me, what did you think of Isabel's impromptu speech last night?"

◄ "Joe, I see you had a paper route as a kid...so did I. Tell me, what did you like the most about delivering papers?"

Small talk also gives you the opportunity to assess the candidate's general communication style and how he or she will fit in with co-workers and your organization's work environment.

5. Take notes!

As you bring out your interview schedule and note pad, take a moment to explain why you will be taking notes. You can say something like:

"Carl, I'm going to be taking notes—it's my way of making sure that I get all the accurate information I need. Please don't let it bother you."

If during the interview you find you need an extra moment to finish writing down some important information then simply explain why you need some additional time. You can say something like:

"Carl, I need an extra moment so that I can get this information down. You've just made an interesting point and I want to be sure that my notes will help me remember all that you said."

As you take notes, focus on summarizing the candidate's key points to your questions, and certainly don't try to copy everything word for word. You don't have that kind of time. Instead, write enough detail so you can later compare the candidate's responses to your skill definitions. Then you'll be able to decide if the candidate has the skills you've identified as being necessary for the job.

Here's an example: You ask the candidate to describe how he or she handled an angry department manager who wanted a report immediately. Your notes might look like this:

Has a system for dealing with angry people—lets the person talk, doesn't interrupt, and when the person calms down, begins to ask what the person would like to have happen. I like this approach!

It is important that your notes accurately reflect what the person said, and provides enough detail so you can recall the important parts of the discussion.

I do not, however, recommend recording the interview. That puts a great deal of extra pressure on the person being interviewed and raises questions about the future or possible uses of the tape.

6. Ask general, open-ended questions.

A good opening procedure is to quickly review your notes, taking a moment to glance at your notes or at the candidate's resume. Then, look the candidate in the eyes, smile, and say something like:

"Greg, you have an impressive background and we're pleased to have this opportunity to talk. It would help me if you could talk to me about what it is you do best."

It is common for interviewers to begin the interview with, "Tell me a little about yourself." Dreaded by most candidates, this question commands thought, preparation, an understanding of the employer's needs and good communication skills.

The savvy candidate will have prepared a clear, brief statement that will highlight his or her pertinent experiences and launch the interview into a positive direction. You may want to ask this question to gauge your candidate's poise and ability to sell his or her skills.

In addition, these general, open-ended questions will raise other questions that you hadn't thought to ask. Jot these down on your list as the interviewee talks.

7. Don't get off-track (too much).

It's natural for other topics and questions to come up. You should feel free to explore these areas. But your interview schedule (your list of questions) must be followed with each candidate so you can compare responses to the same questions. Be sure to return to our list frequently to confirm that you've gathered all the information you need.

Because none of us are born with the natural talent to interview well, you might find some candidates rambling. Sometimes this rambling is due to nervousness. Sometimes it's because they haven't prepared and really don't know what to say next. You need to stay in control. You don't want to be rude, but you don't want to waste time, either. Say something like:

"Ramon, that's an interesting story, but now I'd like to get back to your job experience. Tell me about...."

You can be tactful and maintain control of the interview at the same time, moving it along so that you get the information you really need.

8. Probe to clarify understanding.

Sometimes you have to ask probing questions before you receive the specific examples of how candidates have handled certain situations in the past.

You may need to prompt candidates for specifics, and give an example of the kind of detail you want. Here's how asking for specifics follows naturally from an open-ended question:

"Jon, your comments on your management practices have given me a great deal of general information. Now I need you to get more specific. Think back to a time when you had to ask your people to come in on a Saturday morning to complete a project and exactly what you did, and how it worked out."

Here's another example:

"Jon, it will help me we can get at some information that's more specific. Take your time to think of a situation when you disagreed with your boss about how to organize and manage a project, and tell me what you did."

Key phrases you can use to probe for specific information include:

◄ "Tell me about a time..."

◄ "Describe a situation..."

◄ "Tell me how exactly you dealt with...?"

◀ "It will help me if you can describe in more detail how you handled that."

◀ "Think of a specific time you...and then tell me about what you did."

Advice: Don't be afraid of silence. It can happen. As you ask for specific performance related examples there may be several periods of silence while the candidate recalls just the right example to tell. Silence can work for you, rather than against you. Relax, sit back, and give the person time to think and formulate their responses. You can say something like:

◀ "That's okay, Jennie, take your time."

◀ "Jim, it's all right to take some time to think of the right example. Just take your time and let me know when you're ready."

◀ "You have lots of time, Amy, so don't feel rushed. You'll think of a good example."

You need information from each candidate in order to make a great decision. Sometimes gathering that information means probing, asking for clarification, and even more information—and then waiting while the person recalls.

9. Challenge your hunches.

The interview is going great, the person is easy to talk with and seems relaxed and you're beginning to get the idea that this person walks on water. In fact, if you could, you'd make the offer right now.

When your enthusiasm gets high, it's time to slow it down. A one-sided picture of a person, either all good or all bad, means it's time to ask for contrary information. Why?

When interviewers begin to get a one-sided impression of someone they tend to ask questions that will confirm the impression. The "gut feeling" begins to work and decision-makers often tell themselves "This is the right person, I can just feel it." The interview continues in subtle ways that serve to confirm the "hunch," without digging for depth information. It works both ways.

When an interviewer thinks a candidate has all the wrong skills or behaviors, interviewers tend to ask questions which confirm that impression. Sometimes what is really needed is to just step back and ask for contrary information.

For example, if all the questions have asked for details on situations that went right, you can ask a few questions focusing on situations where things didn't work out. If you are thinking this candidate is truly "walking on water," then it's time to ask for contrary information. You can say something like:

"Pam, this has been really helpful and you have a good track record of dealing with difficult people. Can you think of a time when what you did with an angry customer didn't work, and tell me about it."

If you're thinking this candidate is a real loser, stop and ask for contrary information. You might say something like:

"Al, you've been real candid about why you got fired from your last two jobs. Think of an assignment you were given where everything worked out great, and tell me about it."

You might just discover that Al wasn't a loser himself, but had worked for two poor supervisors.

Sometimes after asking for contrary evidence you may change your evaluation of the candidate. Whether contrary evidence confirms or changes your earlier opinion, it will help you get the information you need to make the right decision.

10. Ask for failures.

No one is perfect. Sometimes the kinds of mistakes candidates have made may add important information to your hiring decision. For example, if you ask the question, "Tell me about a time when your recommendation didn't work out," you'll learn more about how and why the candidate wasn't successful in a project. When you add, "Tell me what you did about it," you gather information on how the person deals with adversity.

Asking about specific examples of failures provides more valuable information than if you ask the old standard, "What is your greatest weakness?" Candidates are often coached in how to evade the "weakness" question to turn weaknesses into strengths. When you ask the candidate to tell about a specific situation, however, you receive more usable and direct information. We've all made mistakes. How we deal with those mistakes makes the big difference.

11. Be alert for possible warning signs.

During the interview you may have seen some warning signs. Any of these warning signs may indicate that you stop before seriously considering a specific candidate. Some of these warning signs might be:

◄ The candidate arrives late for the interview and has no legitimate explanation or offers no explanation.

◄ The candidate quit a job without adequate notice.

◄ The candidate demands that you match or exceed an offer by his or her current employer.

◄ There are no verifiable references, or all the references are social references and not work-related.

◄ The candidate reveals confidential information about a previous employer or employee, or gossips about the previous employer.

◄ The candidate has been involved in wrongful termination litigation.

◄ The candidate can't provide specific examples to back up generalized statements.

◄ The candidate bad-mouths a previous employer or boss.

Though none of these red flag examples constitute a "no-hire" decision on its own, each one suggests you stop and do some more thinking and research. The candidate just may not be someone who will fit within your organization, despite having the technical or performance skills needed.

12. Invite the candidate to ask questions.

Before you conclude, invite candidates to ask questions about the position and the company. You can learn a great deal about candidates just by the questions *they* ask. No doubt you realize that the higher the position, the more sophisticated and detailed the candidate's questions should be.

Ask candidates if they have any questions, saying something like:

"Ruben, I've enjoyed listening to your answers to my many questions, and now it's your turn. Are there any questions you have about the job or about the company?"

Give candidates time to think and be prepared to answer each question in as much detail as possible. Candidates who have prepared for the interview will have their questions ready. You can count on them asking more detailed questions about the position. They may want to know why it is vacant, the management style of the work unit, how they would be evaluated, and details about certain duties of the position.

When someone comes prepared with questions, you know you have a serious candidate. Preparation will show in the kinds of questions asked by each candidate.

Good questions by candidates include:

◄ "What is it you want me to get accomplished during the first six months on the job?"

◄ "What will be the biggest obstacles to reaching these goals on schedule?"

◄ "Based on what you said and my past experience, I think I would.... Is this the kind of approach that will work in this environment?"

In some instances it may seem like the candidate is interviewing *you*. That's usually okay. It shows initiative. If the questions, however, tend to focus on procedural items ("How are half-days figured for vacation time?") this may be a red flag that here's someone more interested in perks than in performance.

Candidates who only want to know about sick leave, vacation policy, and raises are more interested in compensation than in finding the place where they can be truly successful and do what they do best. Beware the candidate who only asks about benefits. This person is often the employee who takes each sick-leave day allotted and may argue over whether they have an extra 1.5 hours of vacation due.

13. Close on a positive note.

Closing the interview well is as important as beginning it well. You are still establishing rapport, and you want each candidate to leave thinking that your company is truly an employer of choice. In fact, you want to conclude each interview with the intent that each candidate leaves *wanting to work for you and wanting the job!*

As you close the interview you will:

◄ Thank each candidate for his or her interest in the company and the position. Let the candidate know you appreciate the time taken to talk with you. You can say something like:

"Thanks, Tish, for your interest in working at ABC Corporation, and for taking time to meet with me today. It certainly seems that you have made some fine contributions in the past, and are ready for more. Let me tell you what happens next in our selection process..."

◄ Make certain in your closing comments that you do not make any comment that may later be construed as an offer. Don't even think of saying, "Gee, but your answers were sure a lot better than the other people I've interviewed."

◄ Take the time to summarize the next actions steps for the candidate. Describe for each candidate what the procedure is from this point on, and when you hope to finalize a decision and notify all the candidates. Don't leave people wondering about what to do next or if they should show up for work the next morning. You can say something like:

"Tish, we will be interviewing a total of five candidates and expect to be completed with all of our interviewing by next Friday. Then we will check each candidate's references and plan to have that completed by the tenth of the month. Then we'll make our decision. You can expect to hear from me no later than the fifteenth of the month."

◄ Walk with the candidate to the company entrance or elevator. That not only assists the person in finding the right way out, but is another way of saying, "At this organization we help each other by being considerate and taking time for even small things."

On the way back to your office you can begin thinking about the final action in getting the information you need for a great decision.

14. Gather additional information.

Most hiring decisions for non-exempt or hourly positions are based on a single interview with finalists. For specialized positions or exempt and salaried positions you may want to schedule a second interview with the top two or three candidates. The focus during this second interview is to gather more in-depth information about the person's skills, to clear up or review any topics that remain vague or unanswered from the first interview, and to meet with other company executives or prospective co-workers.

Some organizations use personality and even IQ tests as part of the application process. If you use a personality test, such as the Predictive Index, or a temperament inventory like the Myers Briggs, or even an instrument like the Kolbe Conative Index, which measures how a person naturally gets work done, make certain the test has been researched and measures what it says it measures. No test should have any internal bias for either gender, ethnic origin, or age.

The most effective use of instruments is achieved only when a profile of the natural skills needed to be successful in the position has been developed. This process involves an analysis of both top performers and weak performers in the targeted position. Key people who will relate to this position also need to be consulted as to the skills they perceive are necessary to be successful. This preferred profile can then be matched with the profiles of top candidates. Developing this preferred profile takes time and money, and is best accomplished by someone with experience. Testing, however sophisticated, is still only one part of the entire hiring process, and are one more piece of information along with the review of the candidate's past experiences and the face to face interview.

What about drug testing? This is a highly controversial topic. A general rule that has been very workable is to apply drug testing only to those kinds of positions in which safety of the public or other co-workers might be involved.

15. Review the interview.

Now that you have the information you need to make a great hiring decision you must take time to summarize your findings in a way that will help you evaluate each candidate. The best time to do this is right after the interview. If you wait even a few hours you may unintentionally forget some important aspect of the interview. The best strategy is to plan your schedule so that when the interview is over you have time to:

1. Review your notes, and make appropriate changes or additions.

2. Compare the candidate's skills with the previously identified technical and performance skills.

3. Summarize your findings in enough detail so that later you can objectively review and analyze all of the candidates at the same time.

The candidate evaluation form (introduced in Chapter 2 and reviewed in Chapter 7) will help you summarize what you've learned from each candidate so you can make an effective hiring decision. When you take time right after the interview to summarize your findings using the chart, then you'll be ready to evaluate and select, based on more than a gut feeling.

First, review your notes, focusing on the headings for each of the technical and performance skills identified. Write brief notes for each of the categories on the candidate evaluation form in enough detail so you can accurately recall your assessment of the candidate's skills in relation to the requisite skills.

Second, indicate whether you believe the person either has the existing skills to fit within your organization, can grow into the organization, or wants something far different than what will be found within your organization.

Here's an example: Candidates A and B have all the technical and performance skills needed to be successful in the job. However, you're moving your organization to self-directed teams and both A and B said they didn't like the accountability of self-directed teams. Because you've learned the hard way that employees need to support the concept of self-directed teams to make them successful, your notes will indicate that A and B just may not fit. The information will be taken into account later when you do your final analysis and make your hiring decision.

Third, review your candidate evaluation form once more. This is to be an objective summary of which candidates have the requisite sills and what strengths each candidate might bring to the organization. Your summary information needs to be objective and in enough detail so that later, when you make your hiring decision, your decision will be based on valid information.

Chapter 6

▲▼▲

Stay on the Right Side of the Law

There are some questions you can't ask. Federal legislation and guidelines are designed to eliminate discrimination in the workplace so there is equal opportunity for all based on skills and abilities, not on bias and prejudice.

When you avoid asking discriminatory questions, or questions that have nothing to do with a person's ability to do the job, it not only keeps you out of trouble with the regulators, but it also shows that you're an organization that values people and makes decisions based on skills.

Your hiring decisions must be based on BFOQ. The term has been around for a long time, and it stands for *bona fide occupational qualification.* Federal guidelines state that you cannot base a hiring decision on anything other than a *bona fide occupational qualification.* This means your hiring decisions are based on a match between those skills needed for the job and the qualifications of the candidate. You cannot *not* hire because of age, gender, marital status, race, religion, disability, or sexual preference in some states.

There are related questions that may be construed by others as gathering information that has nothing to do with a person's qualifications. Too many managers try to get around the standards by asking related questions. For example, while it's clear you can't ask how old a person is or when the person was born, some managers will ask, "When did you graduate from high school?" That question, however, can be construed as asking about age.

Questions to avoid

Here are examples of questions to strike from your interview list. Ask them and they may get you and your organization in difficulty. Focus on BFOQs instead and you'll enhance your organization's standing in the workplace.

Age-related

You should not ask:
◄ How old are you?
◄ When were you born?
◄ When did you graduate from high school?
◄ When did you graduate from college?

The only question you can ask about age is whether the person is 18 years or older. (In most states, child labor laws no longer apply to workers 18 and older.) Questions? Consult employment law counsel.

Marital and family status

A great deal of discrimination occurs in the areas of marital and family status. Questions you should not ask include:

◄ Are you married?

◄ Do you intend to get married soon?

◄ Do you have children?

◄ Are you a single parent?

◄ Do you practice birth control?

◄ How many people live in your household?

◄ Do you live by yourself?

◄ Do you have someone who can take care of a sick child?

It always amazes me when women report that they've been asked, usually by male managers, intimate questions about their personal lives that have absolutely nothing to do with the job. Don't even think about asking personal kinds of questions. If you do you'll probably find yourself in hot water, and your organization will find it difficult to hire the top people.

Remember, however, if the job requires certain kinds of activities, it is fair to ask about the person's ability to meet those job requirements. For example, if the job involves overnight travel you can ask about the candidate's ability to meet that requirement. Let's say the job regularly involves overnight air travel about one-third of the time. You can then ask each applicant something like this: "As you know, the job involves 30 percent overnight travel—would this be a problem for you?"

Ethnic origin

Though it might be interesting to know a particular candidate's history, unless it has a bearing on the job, then don't talk about it during the interview. Questions to avoid include:

◄What's your nationality?

◄Where are your parents from?

◄What languages do your parents speak?

◄Do you speak English at home?

◄Is English a second language for you?

◄What's the origin of your name?

If a job requirement is to speak another language, then you can ask if the person is fluent in that specific language. As more companies engage in world-wide commerce knowing other languages may be a plus for the candidate. Otherwise, asking questions about ethnic origin and race are not acceptable in today's workplace.

Religious and political preference

Unless it's for a particular religious or politically related position, there is no reason to ask any of these kinds of questions:

◄What do you do on Sundays?

◄What church are you a member of?

◄Is that a Jewish name?

◄Do you sing in the church choir?

◄Do your children go to Sunday School?

◄Is there any day in the week you're not able to work?

◄Are you a member of any religious group?

◄Who did you vote for in the last election?

◄How are you registered as a voter?

If the position involves working at a time when many people in the community attend religious functions you can ask each applicant something like this: "The job involves working each Sunday from 7 a.m. to 3 p.m. in the afternoon. This is a basic job requirement for this position and there are no exceptions. Would you have any difficulty in meeting this work schedule on a regular basis?"

Otherwise, there is no reason to inquire about a person's religious or political beliefs. Think BFOQ.

Disabilities

If it doesn't have anything to do with a person's ability to do the job, then don't ask a question designed to reveal information about a disability:

◄ What health problems do you have?

◄ Do you have any disabilities?

◄ Are you physically fit and strong?

◄ Is your hearing good?

◄ Can you read small print?

◄ Do you have any back problems?

◄ Have you ever been denied health insurance?

◄ When were you in the hospital the last time?

◄ Do you see a physician on a regular basis?

◄ Do you have large prescription drug bills?

Some companies may try to ask similar kinds of questions during the hiring process so they can keep their healthcare benefits costs down. Don't even think of it.

You can, however, ask questions about physical qualities that deal with the job. If the job requires the employee to lift up to 50 packages per day, which weigh up to 30 pounds each, you can say to *each applicant interviewed*: "This job involves a lot of lifting. Are you able to consistently lift up to 50 packages per day that weigh up to 30 pounds each?"

Two basic guidelines

Two basic guidelines will help keep you on the right side of the law when interviewing prospective employees. Keep these two guidelines in mind as you prepare and conduct your interviews and you won't get yourself or your organization in difficulty.

1. Craft only questions that help you decide if the candidate has the right skills and experiences to be successful in the position. This means you follow the time-honored BFOQ paradigm. It's been around for a long time, and for good reason.

The questions listed in this chapter are not all of the questions you should *not* ask, but they give you an extensive sampling of the types of questions that might be considered discriminatory. Remember, you can't ask questions other than those that directly relate to the qualifications needed to be successful in the position.

2. Ask each candidate the same questions as they relate to any area that someone might consider to be bias-based. And, in your notes you need to show that you have asked all interviewed candidates the same questions.

Let's return to the overnight travel example: If the job requires 30 percent overnight travel, then you need to ask *each candidate* if he or she can consistently meet that job requirement. If you ask only those people whom you think have a family, or you only ask women if overnight travel is a problem, you open yourself for a possible discrimination complaint. In addition, it certainly won't help to position your organization as a top employer.

Remember: When there are certain valid requirements for the job you can ask questions that otherwise might be considered discriminatory (such as overnight travel, or ability to lift packages) but you must do it very carefully—and you need to ask *each* applicant the same question or questions.

If you have any doubt about a specific job qualification and how to determine if applicants can meet that job qualification, then be certain to seek your company's legal counsel for their advice.

How do you stay on the right side of the law? Easy. If the question doesn't have anything to do with the job and the candidate's ability to successfully perform the job tasks and function, then don't ask it.

Chapter 7

▲▼▲

Evaluate and Select With Confidence

Interviews with the top candidates are finally concluded. Now it's time to return to your notes from the top interviews. When you have a system for evaluating candidates the decision-making process takes less time and is made with more confidence than when you just rely on your intuition or hunch. Here is how you can make your decision more effectively:

Use your candidate evaluation chart

The candidate evaluation form at the end of this chapter provides an efficient way to organize your thoughts and reactions to each candidate. With this tool, you can review each candidate objectively, and identify the person who will be the most successful in the position and within your organization. If you completed your chart after each interview then you're ready to move to selection. If you didn't, then complete your chart now.

First, review your summary statement about the position, focusing on both the technical and performance skills needed to be successful.

Second, review your notes from each candidate's interview. Don't hurry—spend enough time with each candidate so that you can recall what was talked about.

Third, make your notes on the candidate evaluation form. Add enough detail so your summary chart can adequately and accurately summarize the strengths of each candidate. Remember you're working with both technical and performance skills areas.

Your forms might look something like those at the end of this chapter.

Complete your reference checks

You probably asked for references as part of the application process and now is the time to make use of them. If you interviewed only three or four people, you'll probably want to check each person's references. Though many employers are unwilling to provide information other than dates of employment, checking references can still be worth the time and effort.

The purpose of checking references is to not only verify the information you received about the candidate but to gather even more information. Some people also use reference checking as a way to "test" their own perceptions of each candidate. All of the information can be used when you make your final decision.

Information from references that will help you make great hiring decisions include:

◄ How long have you known this person, and how?

◄ Have you worked with this person before? Where? How?

◄What are this person's strengths?

◄How is this person regarded by peers?

◄What is one thing this person needs to work on?

◄Why would you hire this person?

Checking references is one more way to help you base your hiring decision on more than just a gut feeling.

Review your notes and make your decision

The candidate evaluation chart has been filled in, references have checked, and now it's actually decision time. What next? You begin to analyze your findings, looking for the person with the skills that match your job needs the most clearly, and who will fit in with your organization.

Making that final decision must be more than just a gut feeling. Gut feelings too often lead to high turnover and costly mistakes. Whatever system you use to make that final analysis and decision must be objective, fair, and applied to all candidates.

Time to make an offer

Your first call will, of course, be to the successful candidate as you make the company's offer. This usually involves an offer over the telephone followed the same day by a letter detailing the offer. The offer in writing should include details about job title, compensation, start date, and other terms that may have been discussed and need clarification.

Allow time for the candidate to review the offer. How much time? It depends on the position. The general practice is that the lower the position the less time a candidate is given to say yes or no. For management positions several days is fairly standard, again, depending on the exact level and location of the position. If you need the position filled quickly then let the finalist know that you need to confirm the position as soon as possible.

Don't drive away top candidates, however, by insisting they give you an answer "right now, today." They may say yes under pressure, only to back out several days later because a better offer was available, or they felt pressured and didn't like the implication of working under pressure.

Sometimes candidates will make a counteroffer. Some companies expect to negotiate the final offer at all levels, while others negotiate only for managerial and executive positions. Still other organizations make it clear from the beginning that their first offer is their best and final offer—for all levels. You will have to decide which approach works best for your organization. If you choose to have your first offer be your best offer then tell the successful candidate either during the interview process or when you make the offer.

If you decide that negotiating the final agreement fits with your position as an employer of choice then be ready to discuss the final arrangement. Candidates are often coached to counter with a salary figure higher than what they expect to actually receive. Or, they may counter with a request for enhanced benefits, such as longer vacation, better healthcare coverage, and professional memberships.

Sometimes it's advantageous to the organization *not* to negotiate salary but to give a hiring or signing bonus instead. A hiring bonus is not considered annual salary and future raises are not based on salary plus the hiring bonus. Sometimes other perks are negotiated, such as vacation, travel allowance, memberships, and so on. My suggestion: As long as the counteroffer is within reason, continue to negotiate. If you reach the limit in salary and benefits, tell the candidate directly.

If you'd like more information on negotiating check your local bookstore, and look for the National Press Publication *Successful Negotiating* or *Roger Dawson's Secrets of Power Negotiating*, published by Career Press.

Once the candidate has officially accepted the offer, then follow up with a confirmation letter. This correspondence should express the company's pleasure to welcome the new employee, as well as reiterate the start date, compensation, and job title—not to mention any changes to terms renegotiated between offer and acceptance.

Here's an example:

Dear (Name)

Welcome to the team! We're glad you've agreed to join Widget Enterprises as our newest Stock Puller.

As we had talked on the phone earlier today, you will begin work here at Widget Enterprises on January 15th. When you arrive look for the special parking area for new employees. You'll find a spot with your name on it to use your first day! Come to our main entrance, give your name to our receptionist Elaine, and she'll call Hank from Inventory Management. Hank will introduce you to your new co-workers and answer any questions you might have.

After you've been introduced to your new co-workers Hank will bring you to my office and your orientation to Widget Enterprises will begin. We're sure you'll like working here—the job, the people, the surroundings. Your starting salary will be $11.90 per hour with a performance review in six months, at which time you'll be eligible for a pay increase. Hank can answer any questions you have about our compensation program.

Again, we're glad you chose to be part of our team at Widget Enterprises. I think you'll find this an exciting place to work and we'll do all we can to insure your success in this and future positions with us.

Sincerely,

(Name of manager)

Would you be impressed if you got this kind of letter after you accepted your first "real job" after school? Of course you would—and you'd show it to your parents and friends, too. Does a letter like this have an impact? You bet it does! It sends the message that you're glad the person is coming to work at your organization, that you have a plan to help the employee get introduced to the work and the work environment, and that you want the person to be successful.

Not many of your competitors send letters like this.

Notify the others, too

What about those other candidates you talked with? Or those who applied but didn't get interviewed? Of course, you'll want to wait until your top candidate accepts—or declines—your offer first. That way you have the opportunity to offer the job to the next-in-line.

If you want to enhance your company's reputation in the marketplace, then send the interviewed candidates *personalized* letters. Let them know that you appreciate their interest in your organization and you value the time they took to talk with you about the organization's needs.

A general rule to follow: Treat all applicants like they might be your own next boss. They'll remember the excellent, affirming treatment they received from your organization and they will pass the word.

You also need to send letters to those who applied but who didn't make it to the finalist role. This letter will enhance your company's reputation in the marketplace and position your organization as a great place to work. This letter needs to be well-written, attractive, and give the applicant reasons to remain interested in your company.

On the next page are letter samples: the first, targeted to applicants who were interviewed, and the second to applicants who were cut before the interview stage.

▲▼▲

Dear (Name)

Thank you for your interest in the position as Stock Puller here at Widget Enterprises. We appreciate your interest in being part of our employee team, as well as the time you have given as we evaluated several top candidates.

Our offer has been accepted by another candidate. Though you have many of the skills we believe are important to be successful in the Stock Puller position, we found the other candidate to have even more of the skills and experience we need at this time. We were impressed, though, with (add a personal touch here, a phrase about one of their major strengths)

We will keep your application on file for the next six months and will contact you if an opening occurs which calls for a person with your skills and experience. Please call me directly if you believe you are qualified for any of our future openings.

Again, thank you for your interest in Widget Enterprises. We all wish you well in your pursuit of a position that makes full use of your many skills and abilities!

Sincerely,

(Name of manager)

Dear (Name)

Thank you for your interest in the position of Stock Puller with Widget Enterprises. There were many applications and it was not an easy decision as to the people we would interview.

Though it appeared from your application that you had some of the skills we need for the position there were others who even more closely fit the profile of what it will take to be successful in that job.

Your resume will be kept on file for the next six months (or however you handle applicant resumes). If there are other positions here at Widget Enterprises for which you believe you have the necessary qualification, please contact us.

Again, thank you for your interest in our company. I wish you well in your search for a position in which you can be successful.

Sincerely,

(Name of manager)

▼▲▼

Remember, you want your company to attract top candidates—and one way to gain this reputation is to treat everyone who applies with regard and consideration. It doesn't cost—it pays.

Candidate Evaluation
Technical Skills

Candidate	PC Skills	Wonder Widget Production Machine	Regular Maintenance	Identify What Is Not Working	Fix What Is Broken	Portable Phone	Other

Candidate Evaluation
Performance Skills

Candidate	Work with Operators, Supervisors, Managers	Continuous Change	Deal With Emergencies	Stay With It Until Finished	Team Member	Interact With Other Departments	Learn New Technical Skills	Other

Chapter 8

▲▼▲

How Do
I Handle the
Unexpected?

What do you do when a candidate-from-hell somehow gets through? When all the planning and preparation doesn't seem to come together? You deal with it, of course, as best as you can. The important thing is not to lose control. Even in dealing with the unexpected you want to think in terms of positioning your organization as an employer of choice. You may be able to turn the unexpected into a positive.

Here are several situations that sometimes occur—with specific suggestions on how to effectively deal with them.

What if the candidate is late?

Ted put on his freshly cleaned suit, put his resumes and notebook into his briefcase, and left DeKalb in plenty of time to arrive for his interview in Chicago's downtown Loop. Halfway down the toll road, however, the transmission went out on a three-month old car. It happens.

Even though candidates are typically advised to arrive at least 10 minutes early for an interview, sometimes they are late. Events beyond their control do take place, and though the candidate tries, he or she just can't get there on time.

The responsible candidate will call to advise you that he or she will be late, and ask if you prefer to reschedule the entire interview. Hopefully the call can be made before the time of the interview, so you can go ahead with other activities.

What if the candidate is 15 minutes late and hasn't bothered to call? That fact becomes part of your information about the person's performance. You'll want to know why the candidate was late, and provide time for the candidate's explanation. Remember, sometimes you need to seek contrary evidence and, during the interview, ask for more detail about the person's record of being on time.

If the candidate is late, don't jump to conclusions either way. Proceed with the interview. You need more information before you decide if the late arrival is an important factor.

What if the candidate won't talk?

There are people who become so nervous during an interview that they just can't seem to think of what to say, or they become so tense they can't speak. Instead of talking, they sit and say nothing. How do you handle this unexpected situation?

Remember that part of your goal during the interview process is to help the company enhance or maintain its image as being "a great place to work." This means that you won't put the person down, or make light of the situation. Instead, you will treat the candidate with regard and as much empathy as you can.

You can say something like:
"Sam, that's okay. Take your time in thinking about what you want to say. When you're ready, go ahead and tell me about your last job. Would you like a cup of coffee?"

Sometimes candidates find it helpful and easier to talk if they have something in their hands. This is particularly true of people whose strengths are in working with their hands, or with tool or machines. A cup of coffee or a soda provides something to handle, and often that relaxes the candidate. If, for whatever reason, the candidate just isn't able to continue with the interview, ask if the person wants to reschedule.

What if the candidate won't stop talking?

It is often more challenging to deal with the candidate who simply won't stop talking. You ask a question and they answer...and answer...and answer. It wouldn't be so bad if the things they were talking about had anything to do with the question you asked.

Your task, then, becomes assisting those talkers in maintaining focus. You can wait for the person to pause, but sometimes you may have to jump in and interrupt. You can say something like:
"Tom, that's an interesting story, but I would like to focus on how your experience and skills apply to the job needs here at Wonder Widgets. Let me re-phrase my question so you can give me some specific information."

If, after your best moves to get the person back on the topic, the person continues to ramble, make a note of it, and bring the interview to a close. The person obviously won't fit into your situation and there is no need to use your time to listen to things you don't care about. Next, please.

What if the candidate can't provide examples?

Sometimes candidates, in the nervousness of an interview, just can't recall specifics. Try to:

◄ Coach the candidate, by giving an example of the depth of information you're looking for.

◄ Refer to the person's resume, and ask for specific information about a particular item.

◄ Let the person talk in generalities for a brief time, and try again asking for specifics.

To get the candidate back on track, you could say: "Jason, I know that sometimes it's not easy to recall specifics. I want to give you the opportunity to present yourself as best you can. Let me give you an example of the detail I'd like. On your resume you reported that you designed and implemented a computerized preventive maintenance program. One of the things I'd like you to tell me about are the steps you took to develop this program and what were some of the results of the program once you had it up and working."

If the candidate still cannot provide specific example, you will need to make a decision. Is this a case of interview jitters—or is this a sign that the candidate cannot understand direction?

What if the candidate has misled you?

If you begin to realize that the candidate has misrepresented himself or herself during the application and screening process, you need to quickly decide:

◄ Did the person not fully understand the position and the requisite skills and experience?

◄ Did the person get overly ambitious in describing his or her skills and experience, or fabricate accomplishments?

◄ Is the person someone whom you suspect regularly misrepresents the truth?

Probing questions can assist you in deciding if the person hasn't been totally honest in the application and screening process—or perhaps misunderstood some instructions or questions.

Ask for information to help clarify your feeling. If you believe the person didn't fully understand the position announcement, you can say something like:

"Steve, it seems that you and I are talking about two different kinds of jobs. From your description of your past performance, it just doesn't seem that what you listed on your resume really applies. Perhaps we need to close this interview, and I can tell you how to apply for other positions here at ABC Corporation..."

If you believe the candidate misrepresented information in the application process you can say something like:

"Steve, it seems that you may have been overly ambitious in describing some of your past responsibilities and accomplishments on your resume - and your skills and experience aren't what we need for this specific position. I think we need to bring this interview to a close. We do appreciate your interest in Widget Enterprises."

Remember that you are still working to position your organization as an employer of choice. Choose your words carefully so that the person leaves thinking to himself or herself, "Gee, I really blew that one...and they seem like such a great place to work."

What if the candidate is unqualified?

From time to time you may get to the interview process and realize, for a variety of reasons, that the candidate is totally unqualified. Remembering the need to maintain the company's reputation as "a good place to work," you can say something like:

"Hernando, it seems fairly clear that your skills and experiences are not what we need for this position. Although you have some fine qualities, your skills don't match with our needs. I appreciate the time you've spent talking with us, and if you're interested, let me tell you how to apply for other positions here."

When addressing this sort of situation, it is important that you:

◄ Are direct in stating that the person does not have the needed skills and experiences.

◄ Are courteous in what you say.

◄ Focus on the requisite skills.

◄ Not say anything that can be taken as an indication that you based your decision on anything other than a BFOQ. (See Chapter 6.)

If the person has other technical and performance skills that might be of interest, then mention these and offer to assist the person in applying for another position. If not, then bring the interview to a close.

What if the candidate gets argumentative?

Once in awhile, the candidate gets argumentative during the interview process. The candidate may take exception to something you say, or want to argue over why you asked a certain question. When the candidate is argumentative or verbally abusive, you can say something like:

"Heidi, our interview isn't the time to argue about that point. This is the time for me to gather information about how your skills and experience might match with those needed to be successful in this particular job. I'd really like to continue with our interview, but I'll need your cooperation in this."

If the candidate cooperates you can continue. If the candidate continues to argue, you can bring the interview to a close. Either way, the candidate's behavior is part of the information you've gathered. Review your notes, summarize your findings, and make your decision.

But walk with the person to the front door. You're still taking actions that show that working within your organization means working for the best.

It's not always easy dealing with difficult situations and the unexpected. But expect it. Because it does happen. Your task is to remain in control, and continue to show even difficult people why your organization is an employer of choice.

What if an internal candidate isn't selected?

You need to handle this situation forthrightly but with care and concern.

At the point you realize the internal candidate is not going to emerge as the top candidate pull the person aside for a private meeting. Begin by reviewing the employee's strengths and contributions to the organization. Ask why the person applied for the position, and why the person thinks he or she was qualified. Listen. Take notes. Don't shake your head either in agreement or disagreement.

Then review the technical and performance skills needed to be successful in the position. After a quick review, go back in detail, focusing on those areas in which the employee both meets and is short of the targeted qualifications. Answer each question the employee may have. As you discuss the job needs and the person's qualifications it should become more clear to the employee why someone with other skills and strengths is needed in the position. As we've conducted this kind of discussion with internal candidates we've had them thank us for not letting them get into a situation where they would not be successful.

If the internal candidate applied for the position because the person was bored or wanted a new challenge then shift the discussion to other organizational needs that fit with the person's best skills and major strengths. If the person wants to do more and has the abilities then, find more for him or her to do. You already have a strong employee who will become even more so, and will tell others, "This is the greatest place to work." Find and keep the best.

Chapter 9

▲▼▲

Keeping
the Best

In the past few years I've watched a major company move from being a city's top employer to being regarded in the marketplace as "just average." A position with that company is still considered okay, but people don't rush to work there with the same energy they used to. Several years ago people would gladly wait for months just for the opportunity to be interviewed. Many would take lesser positions just to get inside the company. Once inside, they believed they could move on across and up into the kinds of positions they really wanted.

The organization was known for its great management team, flexible schedules, and learning programs.

Not any more.

The company became so large that its managers couldn't keep up with all the change. Management styles fluctuated from department to department, with an increasing number of executives managing by intimidation. Work schedules became less flexible, and leadership development budgets were cut. Workloads increased.

Profits increased for awhile. Top management was happy. But productivity began to decrease because people didn't enjoy working there as much as they used to. The worst part? The top minds began leaving, or didn't bother to apply. It became more difficult to hire the same high-quality employee the company attracted and hired five years earlier. Recruiting costs went up. Positions went unfilled. Work didn't get done. Frustrations grew.

Across town a smaller company was working hard to grow. Its CEO knew the organization needed high-quality employees, because its client base was changing, the markets were evolving, and new products were emerging.

The CEO set out to hire top minds. He made certain the work environment was physically inviting. He made sure his executive group knew how to coach and develop managers so that employees were productive *and* glad that they worked there. The company's pay scale wasn't the highest in town, but it began to attract the best people.

Why? Because people enjoyed working there! They liked the surroundings, the way they were treated, their co-workers, the work, and the efforts made to help people be successful. They have a waiting list of people who want to work there.

Once you've attracted and hired the best people, you have to work to keep them.

The preceding chapters present the strategies to make successful hiring decisions. This chapter is a brief *introduction* on how to keep the best people once you've hired them. As you read, remember that is an introduction, not a comprehensive and detailed strategy.

To be totally effective you need to not only hire the best people, but also have the kind of work environment that *keeps* the best people. You don't have to pay the most to keep the best, but you do have to be the kind of place where people want to work. Based on our research, and the global workplace research of others, here are three major considerations for keeping the best.

1. Lifetime affiliation

The first consideration is to acknowledge that you can't keep every great person you hire. Some will find new challenges, be led into new directions, find new interests and be approached with offers that no one could turn down. Key people will leave for a variety of reasons. If their leaving has nothing to do with how you manage the organization then instead of worrying about lifetime employment, begin to think in terms of *lifetime affiliation.*

The preferred word is "alumni," according to *Fast Company* magazine's writer Scott Kirsner (August 1998 "Gone Tomorrow?") "Forget all your old ideas about who works for you and how," Kirsner wrote. "The day someone walks out the door doesn't mark the end of your relationship with that person. It marks the start of a new stage in that relationship."

The goal? A lifetime affiliation in which key people—the best people—feel free to return, are informed about your organization's work, and become some of your most enthusiastic supporters.

Sometimes an alumnus, after gaining new experiences and wisdom from another position, decides he or she prefers to be back working with you. This individual knows the organization. You've kept in touch with the alumnus so he or she knows the changes that have been made. The former employee has learned new strategies and made mistakes at someone else's expense and now, even more seasoned, he or she is ready to return. You keep the best.

Often it is an alumnus who can suggest another top candidate that you should be talking with. Because you've kept these former employees informed they know that when they meet the best, where the best can fit within your organization. In this role they are acting as your personal headhunter without the expense. They help you keep the best.

And who knows when an alumnus can recommend your new product or service because you've kept them informed as to the company's emerging activities? There can be no stronger supporter than someone who had been successful within your organization, who voluntarily left for whatever reason, who remains someone you maintained contact with, and who recalls his or her experience with your organization as one of the best.

Communication with alumni can include sending periodic newsletters, announcements of new products and services, annual reports, and even updated lists of alumni. Some companies send out position announcements for key vacancies, hoping an alumnus might return or recommend just the right person to fill the vacancy.

Think in terms of developing this new kind of relationship, one in which people feel they can return, or continue to support your organization.

2. Quality free time

In the past several years there have been a number of strikes and employee actions that have one basic cause: There was no time for personal and family activities. According to newspaper reports, one striking worker at Titan Tire said he had to take a day's vacation so he could go to Easter church services with his family. He had worked six straight weeks without a day off. He was tired.

Tomorrow's employees won't tolerate those kinds of hours. They're not shirkers, as new research is indicating, but they won't tolerate the kind of workplace where there is not time for personal and family activities. They will exit on their own, and no-thank-you, they will not welcome being one of your alumni.

A nephew of mine is a key bank executive, handling major accounts and working directly with corporations to structure their loans and lines of credit. He has personally increased the bank's book of business in significant ways. He enjoys his work. But he's ready to leave. "Sometimes my mind is fried, and I just need time to get away," he reports. He talks about the times when the phone rings Friday afternoon and when he hangs up he has to call home to tell the kids he can't take them to the zoo on Saturday. Instead, he'll be in the office to meet with a client. He will be missed when he leaves and the bank will lose some of the business he took care of. But he wants time for his wife and family.

Recently, WorkLife Design was called in to explore why a company was having such a high turnover in one department. A number of key people had left within the past several months, we were told, and the company wanted to know why. Turnover was running nearly 50 percent and within five months the company had already exceeded its annual recruiting budget. Exit interviews had suggested that turnover had to do with dollars, as several ex-employees reported they would be receiving higher salaries in their new positions.

After conducting in-depth interviews with both current and former employees, it was discovered that money had *little* to do with turnover. Though there were a number of reasons why people had voluntarily exited, one of the most common experiences was that people were working such long hours they didn't have time for personal and family activities. As salaried professionals they were working 10-plus hour days, and putting time in on Saturdays and Sundays.

"It finally got to me," reported one person, "when after working the past two weekends I was told I couldn't leave on Tuesday at 3:30 to watch my son play soccer. I quite on the spot. It was worth it."

Time is of increasing importance to workers, and balancing work, home, learning, and play is a major issue. Juliet B. Schor, in *The Overworked American*, (Basic Books, 1991) documented that the work week is getting longer, and people have less leisure than two decades ago.

If your work culture doesn't allow time for people to have a life outside the workplace you won't be able to attract or retain the best. A growing number of workers won't put up with long hours. They would rather earn less and have more time with family and friends. The big house, the luxury car, the fancy clothes are not as important as home and family. The best talent will not stay if you make inordinate demands on their time, energy, and lives.

3. Personal and organizational growth

The days of managing by intimidation are gone. The days of getting all you can from employees and then dumping them when they're no longer needed are gone.

What keeps the best today is a workplace culture that focuses on growth. Personal growth. Intellectual growth. Skills growth. Organizational growth. Pause in your reading for a moment. Think back to the previous words. Those are all growth items, and the kind of growth people look for will vary.

The organizations that keep the best will be those whose managers focus on growth, who know how to nurture and develop people, and who learn from mistakes. Managing for growth begins with the assumption that people are active constructors, not just pawns within the workplace. People carry an innate drive to create something larger than themselves, to be part of an organization that thrives. People are naturally motivated and empowered to be successful.

Employees will strive to learn new skills when the workplace encourages learning and growth. This doesn't mean that everybody agrees with each other all the time. In many of the organizations that attract and keep the best the people heatedly discuss the most effective ways to get things done. Once the decision is made, the energy gets turned to making it work.

As one worker said about his employer, Bertch Cabinets: "I have never worked with a finer group of people—they really care about their employees." And both the employee and the owner really mean it.

The emerging workplace

My father was born at the turn of the century and was a pioneer and leader in the vocational education and adult-learning fields. He grew up on a rocky hilly farm and put himself through college by working a year and then going to school for a year. It took him seven years to finish college but he did it without any debt. He was a visionary in many ways, but he never could understand my first career change.

"Rich," he used to say, "why can't you just stick with what you've been doing?" What he sometimes forgot was that he had been teaching me, through words and example, that work is supposed to have meaning. Though he never said it in so many words it amounted to this: When there is no meaning in one's work it is time to find new work.

For many people it is important to find meaning in their work. After all, work consumes a great deal of one's time and energy. If it doesn't have meaning, significance, then it becomes tedious and demoralizing.

That was clearly the experience of a young man whose job had been recently eliminated. In the 1980s I co-directed a retraining institute at Drake University for displaced workers. One of the objectives of the program was to encourage people to identify what they wanted to do with the rest of their lives. I remember one young man who kept struggling with the concept. He asked for some extra time and then explained his dilemma.

He wanted to go to law school. But his father and his brothers were all tire builders at a local tire plant His father had been a tire builder for most of his life, and his brothers had gone from high school directly to the tire factory. "Work isn't supposed to be fun," his dad would say. "Just go get a job and earn enough to pay your bills." That was his dad's approach to work and life.

Don rebelled and went to college but could only finance it for two years. Then, in the family tradition, he went to the tire factory. "It's not what I want," he would say, "it's not what gives me any kind of accomplishment" When Don was caught in the layoff he was relieved. It gave him the opportunity to re-think his future. The retraining program gave him some new skills in exploring what provides meaning for him.

What do these two stories have to do with the emerging workplace? A great deal, because the emerging workplace is one in which people find meaning in their work. If they don't find meaning in their work then they'll move on to the place where they can do what they do best and be fully satisfied at the same time.

Organizations that attract and retain the best are those that experience near-zero turnover because they know that "work" means more than simply a paycheck. They understand that people work to feel productive. To learn and grow. To engage with others. To make a difference. To have fun.

This emerging workplace culture comes from the awareness that organizations are made up of people. The worker is a whole rather than a segmented partial person. No longer simply a pair of hands or a body, but a conscious, motivated, and growth-focused being. Work structures and processes are established with that awareness in mind.

The idea of a vital workplace is both very old and quite new. It was the dominant workplace culture when we were still an agrarian society. However, the concept of a vital workplace all but disappeared with the growth of industrialization and scientific management. The new generation is pushing for its re-emergence as the dominant workplace culture.

There are many terms used to describe this work environment: high-involvement workplaces, learning organizations, communities-of-practice, and the natural workplace to name just a few.

How do you learn about this emerging workplace? Here are three resources that have had and continue to impact on the emerging workplace:

1. Ricardo Semler, *Maverick: The Success Story Behind the World's Most Unusual Workplace,* New York: Warner Books, 1993. Tells the story of the transformation of Semco, a large Brazilian based manufacturing company, from a traditional to a self-directed workplace.

2. Peter Senge, *The Fifth Discipline: The Art and Practice of the Learning Organization,* New York: Doubleday, 1990. Describes the five key principals essential for an organization to continuously learn and improve.

3. Marsha Sinetar, *Do What You Love, the Money Will Follow: Discovering Your Right Livelihood,* New York, Paulist Press, 1987. Discusses the role of values and vision for creating the kind of worklife a person wants.

Some additional names frequently associated with the research and practice of a vital workplace include the leadership styles work of Chris Argyris, Edward Lawler's employee involvement systems, and the more fully human organizations and work of Omar Aktouf. The idea of reinventing work or working with soul are also discussed by such people as Matthew Fox, Lee Bolman, Terrance Deal, Alan Briskin, and Terri A. Deems. Others could be added to the list, each presenting similar qualities and characteristics, as well as a few distinct differences.

Although many business magazines and journals carry articles about the emerging workplace, the magazine *Fast Company* is devoted to this kind of high-energy environment that balances work, love, fun, growth, family, and productivity. It's available at most newsstands each month. If you're not familiar with it, then get it. You may not agree with all that's in each issue, or even fully understand it—but you'd better be aware of it.

Fast Company is becoming more of a movement than just a periodical.

What our own research has found is that the people and organizations that seem to be breaking the most new ground, and making the most significant and sustainable changes while reaping respectable profits, are not always the ones writing about it. Instead, they are doing it. Their management model is "management by common sense" and they structure their organizations with a firm and viable respect for people.

As Joseph Sullivan, chair and CEO of VigoroCorp, describes: "We don't invest people with human dignity. Employees have it before, during, and after employment with us. We managers can, however, provide an environment that enhances their dignity."

Phil Carlson, executive for the Scottsdale, Arizona, Chamber of Commerce, stated it this way: "We are in the midst of creating the new workplace and we don't know exactly what it will look like in the year 2005." But it will look different and by the year 2010 it will be considerably different. The next generation will not work just to pay bills. The work must not only have meaning for them but be a part of their total lives.

Why do people work? Status? Just for bucks? Maybe. But it's also to have fun, to feel productive, and to somehow make a difference. Work isn't just an invention of the western world or the 20th century. Not purely economic. Work is fulfillment. Vital.

The emerging workplace will be one in which people find meaning and significance. Where meaning and significance exist they will hire and keep the best.

Interview Planning Guide

The Interview Planning Guide has been designed to help you plan each interview you conduct for a specific position. Respond to each item with the requested information, and place a check mark when your plans are complete for that item.

▲▼▲

_____
Candidate and date of interview

_____
Position

_____
Interview to be conducted by

1. ____Interview scheduled for:

Date _____ Time_____ Location_____

2. ____Brief description of position:

3. ____Position title_____Salary_____

Grade/level_____ Department_____

Begin date_____ Other_____

4.____Notes for rapport-building statements/questions:

5. ____Questions about **technical skills** to be asked of all
candidates:

6. ____Questions about **performance skills** to be asked of all
candidates:

(Attach additional questions if needed)
7. ____Interview review and summary of findings:

8.____Further action

Additional interview_____ Recommend: Yes__No__

Letter to be sent _____ Other_____

▲▼▲

Index